Pendulum

Circling The Square Of Life To Improve Health, Wealth, Relationships, And Self-Expression

By Erich Hunter Ph.D.

© 2015 by Erich Hunter

All rights reserved. No part of this book may be reproduced in any form or by any means, electronic or mechanical, including photocopying, recording, or by any information storage and retrieval system, without permission in writing from the author.

Disclaimer

The information in this book should not be treated as a substitute for professional medical advice, or treatment. Always consult a licensed medical professional. Any use of the information in this book is at the reader's discretion and risk. Neither the author, nor the publisher can be held responsible for any loss, claim, or damage arising out of the use, or misuse, of the suggestions made, the failure to take medical advice, or for any material on third party websites.

Table of Contents

Acknowledgements v
Foreword vi
Introduction viii
What Is Pendulum Healing? 1
How To Select A Healing Pendulum 3
Pendulum Basics 6
Frequencies of Healing (Radiesthetic Color) 8
Healing In Person vs. Distance Healing 16
The Best Times And Frequency To Do A Healing 19
A Basic Pendulum Healing Protocol 20
"Quick Relief" Healing Example 27
What If The Readings Don't Change After A Healing? 29
Healers Ethics 30
How To Write A Healing Report 32
Wealth: Creating Abundance And Prosperity 36
Self-Expression 48
Relationship To Self: Self Love 55
Letting Go Of Attachment To Outcome 63
Does The Pendulum Heal You? 65
The Science Of Pendulum Healing 71
The Magic Of Pendulum Healing 74

Pendulum Commands 78
What To Do If You Don't Have A Pendulum 81
Stages Of Healing 83
Questions From "Circling the Square of Life" Students 86
Pendulum Healing Charts 111
Afterword 128
About The Author 129
Circling The Square Of Life Online Class 130

Acknowledgements

I would like to thank several people for helping me to produce this work. First, I would like to thank my wife Tarra for her love and support of this project. Next I would like to thank these reviewers who provided feedback on the manuscript: Sharron Cuthbertson, Georgina Haul, Mariann Hoffmann and Muhammad Ajmal Syed. I also would like to thank Charlie Wedel of http://5dcreations.com for the cover photo and La Fortunae pendulums http://www.usafortunae.com for the pendulum used in the cover photograph.

Foreword

The title of this book is a play on a concept in life coaching that there are four major areas people are interested in Health, Money, Relationships, and Personal Growth, and an unrelated concept in magic called "The Watchtower" in which the four cardinal points (North, East, South, West), or Four Elements (Earth, Air, Fire, Water) are invoked during the casting of a magic circle. In my work with pendulum healing and my popular e-course, "Circling the Square of Life," I help people in the four major areas, but I do so not with strategy, but with the circular movements of my pendulum, hence the title of this book.

You may ask why is the topic of magic in a book on healing? The answer is simple. In human history "magic" has always been a part of the healing arts. It is only in the last 105 years since the publication of the Flexnor report in the United States (1910) that modern medicine completely abandoned any "magical", "occult", or "esoteric" aspects of healing in favor of the strict materialist paradigm we have today.

Unfortunately, modern medicine "threw the baby out with the bathwater" while striving to transform the healing arts into the healing sciences something was lost. For all its wonders and improvements in care and healing, modern medicine is the third leading cause of death in countries like the United States, and a significant part of the population seeks out alternative treatments since the medical system is not meeting their needs[1].

As more and more people are exploring alternative healing methods that have the aura of "magic" about them many different healing modalities are being tried and explored and pendulum healing is one these "occult" or "esoteric" healing methods that is becoming available to a wider audience of people interested in alternative healing methods.

My explorations into the practice of pendulum healing have shown me one thing: there is more going on in this world, than materialist dogmatists of mainstream medicine would like to admit. The work with pendulums interfaces with the limits of human understanding, particularly in the field of consciousness, and what effects the human mind can have on altering reality. It also brings us right to the edge of what is known about energy, and non-local phenomena normally reserved for the quantum physics. So I urge you to explore this field of study with an open mind, practice regularly and be amazed by the results.

1. Dossey L., Chopra D., Roy R. (2010) "The Mythology of Science Based Medicine" Huffington Post.

Introduction

It has been said that the perfect plan of life involves health, wealth, love, and perfect self-expression. This is known as the "square of life" and is said to bring true happiness. Using the circular movements of our pendulums, we can enhance these areas of our lives while bringing us into alignment with divine will.

This book includes using pendulums for the following

1. Health: techniques for physical well-being and for healing others.
2. Wealth: creating abundance and prosperity.
3. Love: enhancing self-love and creating more fulfillment in relationships.
4. Self-expression: transforming your life path and manifesting ideal work.

Presented here is a revolutionary healing system that goes way beyond just asking your pendulum questions. In this book I explain how to use the pendulum as an actual healing tool to effect massive positive change in your life quickly. Detailed step-by-step instructions are provided to ensure understanding and guide you to success taking all the guesswork out. You will also learn a solid foundation for going forward on your own and expanding this work, while being able to incorporate it with any other healing modalities you may practice.

I am excited to share this system with you and I truly hope that it empowers you to make positive changes both in your life and in the world.

Sincerely,

Erich Hunter Ph.D.

What Is Pendulum Healing?

Pendulum healing is when you use a pendulum to do what is commonly called energy healing, or spiritual healing, to affect positive changes in another person's health and well-being. It works on body, mind and soul of the person being healed.

Traditional dowsing uses a pendulum to find answers to questions. While this plays a role in pendulum healing, it is de-emphasized and is only a relatively small part of the pendulum healing process. Rather than using the pendulum to seek answers on a dowsing chart, the pendulum itself becomes the healing tool.

This form of healing is relatively new. It was developed in the 20th century in France and in Poland. Now it is practiced by a small, but growing, number of people around the world.

How it works is that the healer uses a special healing pendulum. I will discuss selection criteria in a chapter that follows. Then following a standard protocol, the pendulum healer uses the pendulum to transmit "energy" and mental messages called "thought forms" to the person being healed. If the healer is psychic, or clairvoyant, they can use that skill to help them see what needs to be done in the healing, or they can use that ability to provide important information that could help the person to heal.

Finally, if the pendulum healer has other healing skills, or knows other healing modalities, the pendulum can be used to prepare the person for that type of healing, and it can also be used to help the effects of any other type of healing work to be integrated. For example, a pendulum healer could start out with pendulum work, and then transition to Reiki, acupuncture, massage, crystal healing, or any other form of healing all in a single session. Pendulum healing can also be incorporated with standard western medicine.

While it can be an effective stand-alone treatment, the overall effect of pendulum healing is that it speeds up the healing process, and compliments other healing methods making them more potent.

Another use for pendulum healing is to empower affirmations. Many systems of healing use affirmations to cause positive changes, but just saying them repeatedly is often not enough. Many affirmation systems try to get around this problem by having the person do physical actions (e.g. Emotional Freedom Technique/Tapping), or by saying certain phrases after the affirmation. Since pendulum healing is based on principles of positive magic, however, your words gain power and they can effect real demonstrable changes in reality. This makes pendulum healing a much more powerful way to do any type of affirmation work, since it is based on ancient occult principles known for millennia.

How To Select A Healing Pendulum

It is important to select a proper pendulum for healing work. I had a little difficulty determining where to put this chapter, because in order to properly select a pendulum you need to have some experience with radiesthetic color. A topic covered in a later chapter. So you will need to read that chapter to fully understand this one. To get you started, however, here are some general guidelines.

Healing pendulums come in three basic shapes seen in many variations: the Karnak, Isis and Osiris. The Karnak has a bullet-like shape and produces Green- radiesthetic color. The Isis pendulum has cylindrical disks called "batteries" running down the length and emanates radiesthetic White. The Osiris has bowl shaped disks and emanates Green-. Any pendulum that looks like one of these will most likely be a good healing pendulum.

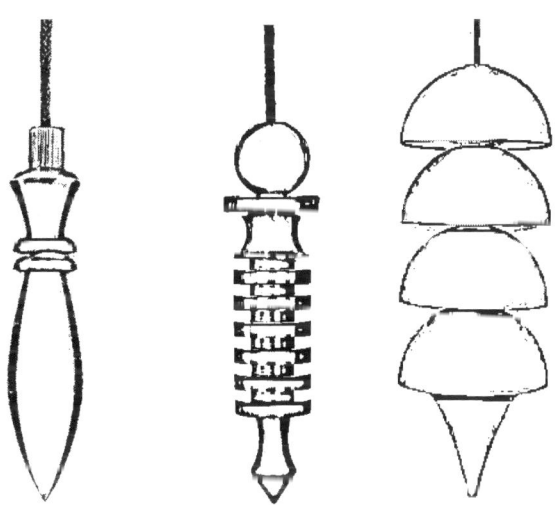

Karnak pendulum, Isis pendulum and Osiris pendulum.

1. Based on experience brass and wood are the best materials for a healing pendulum. It is interesting to note that these two substances have a greater tendency to gain electrons than crystals such as quartz and this could account for their superiority as healing pendulums.

2. Crystal pendulums can sometimes work so if you have one try it out, but based on my experience, crystals tend to be the inferior choice. So unless you already have a crystal pendulum, or you are determined to use one, obtain a brass, or wood pendulum that looks similar to one of the pendulums figured above.

3. A general purpose, healing pendulum should emanate a radiesthetic color of White. A few specialized pendulums will emanate Green–. Read the section on radiesthetic colors to learn how to determine this.

4. Make sure the pendulum feels good to you. Trust your intuition. If it feels solid, and makes you feel confident, test it on the color chart. If emanates radiesthetic White, or Green-, use it. If you can't test it yet, or don't know how, just give it a try. If it works, and you get positive results, use it.

If you buy an inexpensive pendulum off Amazon.com, or Ebay.com it may, or may not, work. If possible, test it against a radiesthetic color chart and if it tests radiesthetic white, or green-, great use it. If not, please don't use it for healing.

You can also make your own pendulum. You can carve one out of wood, or make one out of metal (e.g. metal cylinder, bolt, etc.). Just check it against the radiesthetic color chart.

Pendulum Healing

If you already have a pendulum, and you are not sure if it will work, try it out and see what happens. If you get good results with it, go ahead and use it. If not, take all of the above into consideration and find one that works for you.

Pendulum Basics

You want to grasp the pendulum string with your thumb and forefinger and wrap any extra cord inside the palm of your hand. Make sure that the pendulum can swing freely, while still having a firm grip on it.

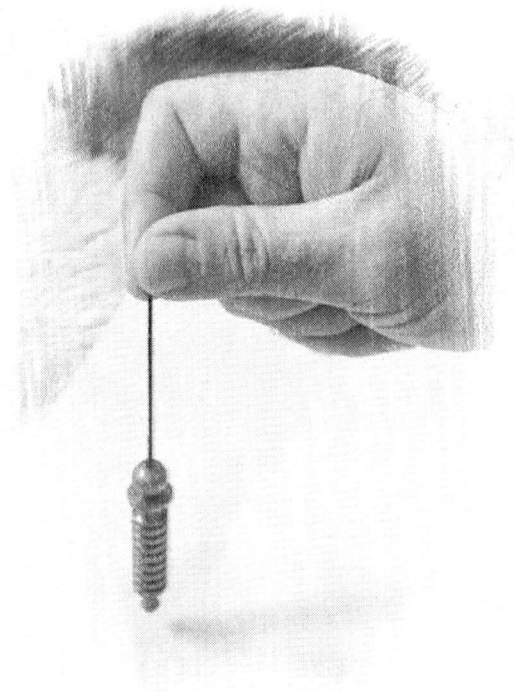

When you are doing a healing you can put it over a person, or over an index card with person's name on it (known as a "witness card"). If you are putting it over a person, you can hang the pendulum over the solar plexus area (which is below the lower ribs, a bit below where they meet), or directly over the area you want to heal. If you are using a witness card, you will just hold it over the card.

Pendulum Healing

Movement of the Pendulum

If done correctly the pendulum will start to move. If it doesn't move, gently move it, but then let it go on its own. Never force the direction of movement.

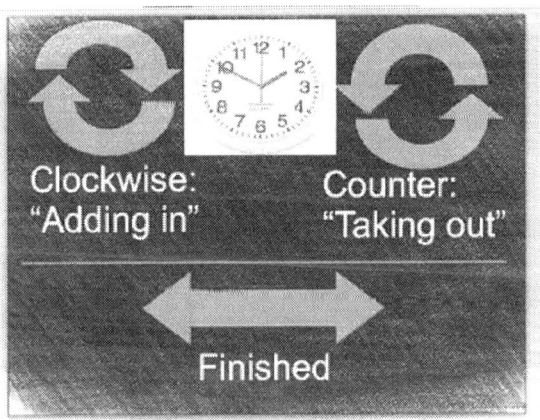

Giving/Receiving/Finished

After you say a command your pendulum will spin in circles. The direction that it is spinning can indicate what is happening. The two basic actions are "giving" where something is being added to the system you are healing, and "removing" where something is being taken away.

When the pendulum is "giving" it will turn clockwise (imagine you are looking at a clock on the wall, clockwise is towards your right).

If the pendulum is "removing" it will turn counterclockwise (to your left).

Once the pendulum is finished it will be balanced and moves side to side.

You don't need to keep track of adding in, or taking out, unless you want to. The main thing is to look for balance (side to side swinging) because it indicates that phase of the treatment is completed.

Frequencies of Healing (Radiesthetic Color)

"In physics, radiation is the emission of energy in the form of waves, or particles through space or through a material medium. This includes electromagnetic radiation such as radio waves, visible light, and x-rays, particle radiation such as α, β, and neutron radiation and acoustic radiation such as ultrasound, sound, and seismic waves. Radiation may also refer to the energy, waves, or particles being radiated."[1]

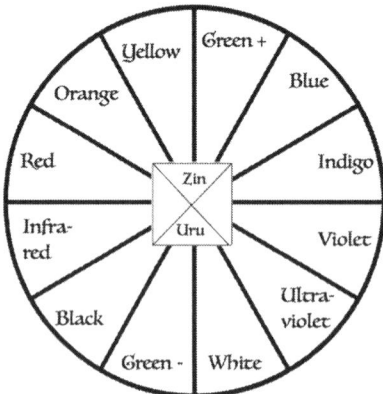

Radiesthetic color chart.

The pioneers of pendulum "science" Chaumery and Belizal believed that pendulums produced emissions that were a form of electromagnetic radiation. They created a scale to describe the emissions that is now called the radiesthetic color scale. The radiesthetic color scale is abstract, yet quite useful for pendulum healing, because it gives a way to measure and name pendulum emanations and detectable "energies" of living beings that we can use for healing purposes.

1. Wikipedia contributors. "Radiation." *Wikipedia, The Free Encyclopedia*. Wikipedia, The Free Encyclopedia, 29 Jul. 2015. Web. 4 Aug. 2015.

For our practical purposes, the chart of radiesthetic color has two uses.

The first purpose is to check the radiesthetic color of the pendulum we are using for healing. A healing pendulum should have a radiesthetic color of Green-, or White.

Hold your pendulum over the chart and say the following pendulum command:

"What is the radiesthetic color of my pendulum?"

Then you dowse the chart and see what color your pendulum indicates is the pendulum's radiesthetic color. In most cases it will swing strongly towards a single color on the chart. In some cases it may indicate more than one color. A typical healing pendulum will indicate White, or Green-. If it indicates another color, do not use it for healing.

The second purpose is to determine the radiesthetic color of a person (or body part) we are healing, and then change the color to Blue.

Hold your pendulum over the chart and say the following pendulum command:

"What is the radiesthetic color of a person/body part?"

"Change the radiesthetic color of the person (or every cell, tissue, and organ) to Blue."

Although this will be explained later, Blue is the radiesthetic color that indicates health.

Now for some explanation about the radiesthetic color chart, with an emphasis on the practical knowledge of what it symbolizes.

I struggled with this section, because in a sense the whole idea of "radiesthetic colors" is very weakly supported by any kind of logical explanation, or experimental proof and if you really think about it the whole notion of using colors is odd, given that pendulum emanations are invisible.

The awkwardness and lack of valid explanation are outweighed by the fact that the concept is extremely useful from a practical standpoint, and the use of colors as a mnemonic device is extremely useful as a memory aide. With that said I am going to explain how I interpret this chart so that it can be of practical value to the pendulum healer.

Here is how to interpret the chart of radiesthetic color:

Green - indicates a person is not well, or won't be well in the near future.

Black, and Infra-red indicate severe illness approaching death.

Red, Orange, and Yellow will not normally show up when dowsing a person's radiesthetic color. They represent the radiesthetic color of the egg/sperm, embryo and fetus respectively.

If you dowse a healthy baby, plant, or someone undergoing rapid cell growth (e.g. growing teenager), it will be Green +.

Blue indicates optimal health.

Indigo, Violet, Ultra-Violet, and White indicate varying degrees of optimal health.

A graphic way to visualize the chart is to view its twelve "radiesthetic colors" as seasons of the year. Spring equinox is the rebirth and the start of life after winter. Summer solstice starts a period of optimal radiant health, life in its full power and glory. Fall equinox is the start of a period of decline and preparation for the oncoming winter. Winter solstice is the start of the final stage where life is put on standstill and death is near. The seeds lie dormant for the rebirth in the coming spring.

Pendulum Healing

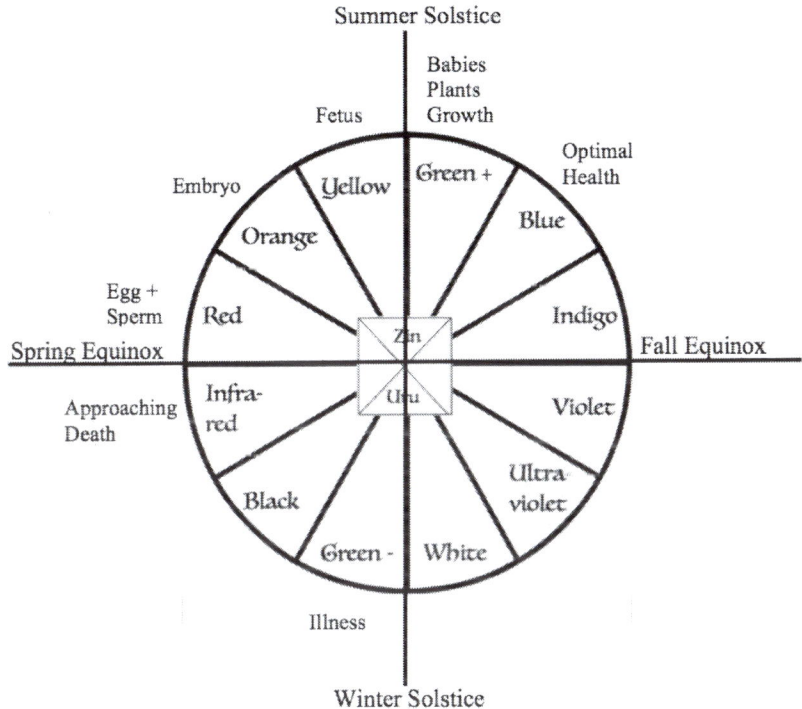

This is a graphic representation of health. When you are in perfect health you are at blue, the height of summer. Fall indicates gradual weakening of health. Illness represents winter beginning of preparation for death, and the rebirth in the next spring.

When reading the chart remember that the radiesthetic color is not permanent and can change over time. Also remember that seasons of life are a natural process, so there is nothing inherently wrong with the current state of health of a person. The chart gives graphic indication to help visualize what is going on.

When you change a person's color to Blue (the color of health), they may or may not get to Blue. This is because the person may not be able to shift into a state of perfect health due to a block, or some other reason, or they may "use up" the energy you are sending them and only get to Blue briefly before losing that state again. Don't worry this is normal.

It is also important to note that radiesthetic color can change again towards "winter colors" after a successful healing. In cases like these, the person may need to do a daily pendulum healing on their own, or you may need to do it for them. If you are doing healing work on a critically ill person, it can help to raise their radiesthetic color on regular intervals over a period of time (say every few hours, or every day, etc.) to help them maintain conditions for regaining health.

You can also, check the chart to see when your healing work is finished. I helped a cancer patient, and after several healings his radiesthetic color improved, even though his health didn't at first. I felt like I couldn't do anymore and every time I checked his color indicated healing (white), so I just waited and then after a couple of weeks his health improved significantly.

Sometimes you will encounter a person who is ill, but they will have a radiesthetic color that indicates they are healthy. You have to vary your healing strategy based on this information.

It indicates that the problems are related to psychosomatic illness, or karmic issues that both can be resolved by reflection and understanding. The approach to both of these issues is similar. You do pendulum work to help the person learn the lessons they need to learn, to move on and to heal. For example here are some useful pendulum commands in this situation:

"Help this person learn whatever lessons they need to learn from this illness."

"Help this person see whatever it is they need to see in order to heal."

As a healer, psychosomatic and karmic cases can be difficult for your ego. This is because these cases will not resolve if a person is not ready to see what the illness is hiding from them, or they may need to suffer through a karmic issue in this lifetime. It is important in these cases to let go of your ego attachment to outcome, and trust that your healing work is helping, even if you don't see a "result." Your healing work may speed up the process of healing "down the road" and it will undoubtedly play some important role in the person's journey of healing. Always have faith in your healing work, even if you see no evidence of result.

How does it happen that a person has a radiesthetic color indicating health, but they are not healthy?

Radiesthetic color is separate from the body. It is like an aura or cloud that gives the body "information" to keep it healthy, but some people can block it so that it has little or no effect. Some people even have the "signal" for health (e.g. Blue radiesthetic color) but they can't utilize it for some other reason (e.g. negativity). These people are in a minority, however. For most people there is a direct correlation between the color and health.

When you change a persons color to Blue it should bring them back to health, but other factors can confound this. In some cases it will be enough to change the color to get a change in health, but in others you may have to experiment with altering other variables (e.g. ability to receive, self love, etc.) to effect noticeable change.

The best analogy I can make is if you are sick and there is medicine in your medicine cabinet you can either choose to take it, or not take it. If you take it you will get better. If you don't take it you could get worse. Radiesthetic color is kind of like that. You can have a health stimulating radiesthetic color (kind of like the medicine in the medicine cabinet) but unless your body utilizes it (i.e. you take it) it won't have any effect.

In my view most pendulum healing is like this. We are putting "energy and thought forms" in the persons aura and they either receive or don't receive this information. Just like you can either take or not take the medicine, but it will still be in your medicine cabinet.

Another way to think about it is that the radiesthetic color is like a map in your car (or maybe a GPS these days). If you follow the map you will find your way. If you don't follow the map you can get lost. The map is always there though.

The weird thing about radiesthetic color (and most other things we are modifying with the pendulum) is that the person creates it, but it also reflects back, and it can be altered by the environment (or by a healer).

Using the map analogy, it is like a person makes a map based on their life stage, health and outside influences, then this map reflects back and they either use, or don't use it. Most people use the map, but people who have good radiesthetic color, but poor health are not using the map, even though it was there.

Most people though have a direct correspondence. If the map is good, they use it and can find their way (e.g. feel healthy). If the map they are making is bad (or if the environment degrades it) they can get lost, or have trouble finding their way (i.e. suffer poor health).

Checking Radiesthetic Color Of Your Environment

When doing a healing, it can help to check the radiesthetic color of your home, bedroom, office, or any place you spend time. If a place where you spend a lot of time is Green-, or Black or Infra-red, it will adversely affect your health.

It can be surprising to learn that your bedroom, or some other place that you go is harmful to your health. This phenomenon is referred to as geopathic stress. If you learn that a particular location is at a radiesthetic color that is harmful to your health, action must be taken to correct the problem, or the health problems caused will continue.

I have experimented with using the pendulum to change the radiesthetic color of a location, but it resulted in only limited success and the radiesthetic color would eventually revert because the underlying problem had not been fixed. It is beyond the scope of this book to explain how to permanently solve these problems of geopathic stress. One thing you can do to help alleviate the problem is to put an Om symbol in the room that has the harmful radiesthetic color. Make sure to use one that does not have a circle drawn around it, or it will neutralize the effect. A computer printout, or hand drawing is fine. You could also sculpt it, or get a tile, etc. The Om symbol will work to continuously to purify the environment of the harmful radiesthetic color. Make sure to check to see if it is working by dowsing the radiesthetic color chart.

Finally, it is interesting to note that trees and growing plants are green + and that is one reason why it feels healing to have plants in your environment, and to go out in nature. If you want an energy boost, find a nice healthy tree and ask it for permission to touch it. If you sit against the tree, or place your hands on it you will absorb the green + frequency. This also explains in part, why women tend to be more in tune with nature than men, because green + is the same radiesthetic color as a healthy baby.

Healing In Person vs. Distance Healing

Before performing pendulum-healing work for another person, you will need to decide if you are going to do the healing in person, or as a distance healing. There is no difference in effectiveness and both methods work. Some people, however, report more dramatic effects from distance healing possibly due to a greater sense of detachment when performing the healing at a distance, while others only work with people in person. It is really a matter of preference.

If you are doing the healing in person, either hold the pendulum over the person's solar plexus, or the body part that is having issues. You can also hold it over a chakra.

If you are advanced, merely holding the pendulum in the air in the presence of the person will work as well. You can also do this for self-healing.

For various reasons you won't always be able to do a healing for someone who is present with you, or you may feel uncomfortable holding a pendulum over yourself. In cases such as these, you can create a "Witness Card" to help you do a distance healing. The simplest way to do this is to write a persons name on an index card, and then hold the card in your hand while saying the persons name 3 times with focused intention. Once done, the card is now "linked" to that person and any healing efforts you make using the pendulum will transmit directly to the person who is being healed.

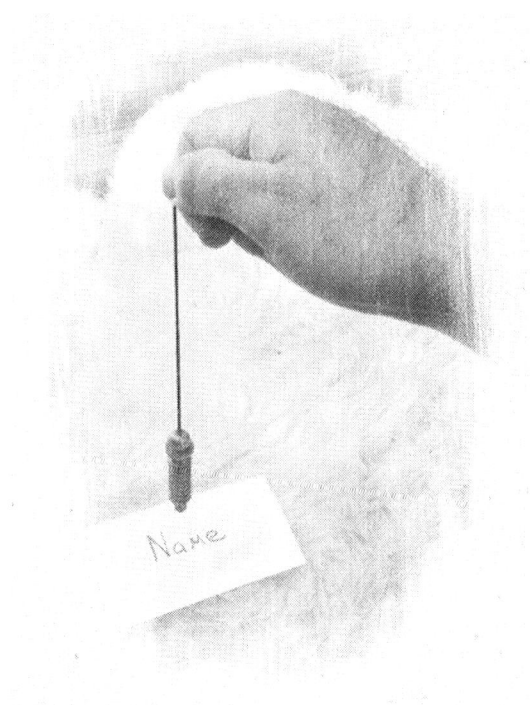

There is no need to use a picture of a person, or a lock of hair. If you link the card to the person in the way described above, any healing actions you do over the card will go to that person. Try to get the name spelled correctly. The most important aspect though is your intention to link the card to the person. Do the healing the same way as you would for yourself, or another, just use the witness card as a substitute for a person.

When you are finished with the healing "disconnect" the card from the person by saying 3 times "Back to your body" and then blow 3x forcefully onto the card.

Some people have asked me if making a witness card is absolutely necessary. It is not. If you have a strong connection to someone, or if you are advanced at doing healing work, you can proceed without making a witness card. However, I do recommend using a witness card if you are just starting out, or if you want to build confidence in distance healing. I use a card for almost all of my healing work, but I don't use one when doing a self-healing. With that said, I recommend using the card, unless you strongly feel that you don't need it.

The Best Times And Frequency To Do A Healing

If possible, try to do your healing work when a person is either sleeping or resting. When a person is resting their guard is down and their subtle body is more open to healing. This doesn't mean that a healing will not work at other times; it is just that periods of sleep and rest are an optimal time. When a person sleeps they can also integrate the healing better, since the body heals during rest.

If a person is actively using a computer, or cell phone, while you are doing a healing it can actually block your healing efforts. Also, if the person is actively engaged in a stressful activity it can also hinder your efforts.

Once you have completed a healing, you may need to do it again. There is no set time for when you should do this.

If the person requests another healing, or asks for help, then that is a good time to assist them. Often a person will feel partial relief from your healing effort and ask you to continue until the issue is resolved (This is especially true for simple cases like a pain, or stomach ache). If you are doing a healing at a distance, you can check in with the person after the healing and offer to help them again if they want.

You can also determine the number of sessions you think they will need, or the frequency of sessions, with your pendulum. The easiest way to do this is to dowse a number line like the one below, or use your intuition.

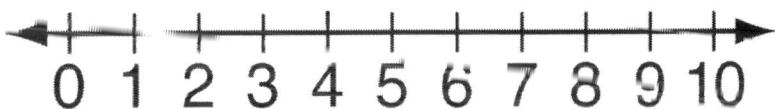

A Basic Pendulum Healing Protocol

In this chapter I will walk you step by step through a pendulum healing protocol so that you can easily do a healing yourself. All you need to do is follow the steps and use the command prompts I have given. I will explain the concepts in other chapters. This is to provide an easy to follow template that will get results immediately.

Step 1: Start your work with a prayer.

Here is a sample that you can use, or you can make your own.

"Dear Higher Power, I surrender this healing to you. I pray that it is in the highest good of myself, and the person I am healing, and all concerned."

You can also invoke the help of spiritual allies and protectors.

Then you can center yourself, relax and get into a "meditative state".

Step 2: Gather information.

>   A) Have the person describe the situation to you in his or her own words.
>   B) Take notes, or have them write it down.
>   C) Look for clues that will help you focus your healing effort.
>   D) See if they provide the solution to their own healing.

Step 3: Reformulate what the person says into positive statements.

Put these positive statements on an index card with the person's name.

For example, the person says "I burned my finger"

Pendulum Healing

You write, "her/his finger is healed" on the index card.

You will use these positive statements in Step 7 of the healing process.

Step 4: Begin the healing by increasing the person's ability to receive.

Increasing a person's ability to receive is a good place to start a healing. If they aren't open to receiving, your healing efforts might not have as much of an effect.

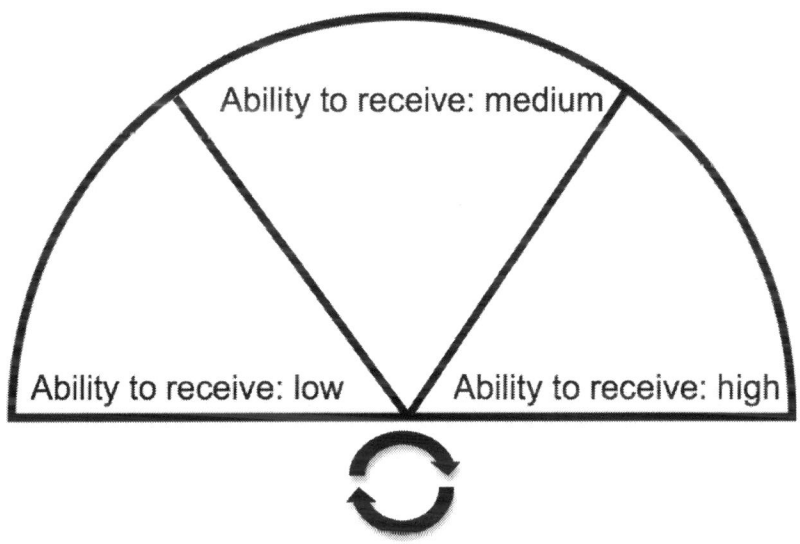

The pendulum command is:

"Increase (the person, or body part) ability to receive to the highest level!"

If you do this correctly, the pendulum will spin over the chart when you finish. That means you have provided excess energy that they can draw from over time. Good work.

If you check them and the pendulum doesn't spin, give it some time to settle out. Check it later. If needed, repeat several times until the pendulum spins.

Step 5: Increase the will to live and vitality

Next you can increase the will, or desire, to live. Note that desire to live is not the same as vitality (which we will do next). Vital people have killed themselves. Increasing the will to live helps ensures the person you are healing (or body part) wants to be around to heal.

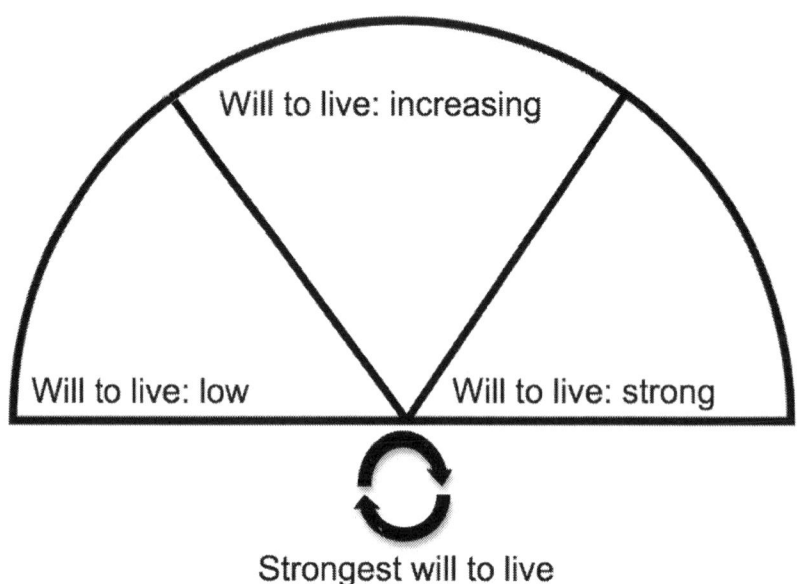

The pendulum command is:

"Change (person/body part) so that (they/it) has the strongest will to live."

Next work on the vitality of the person and any affected body parts.

Pendulum Healing

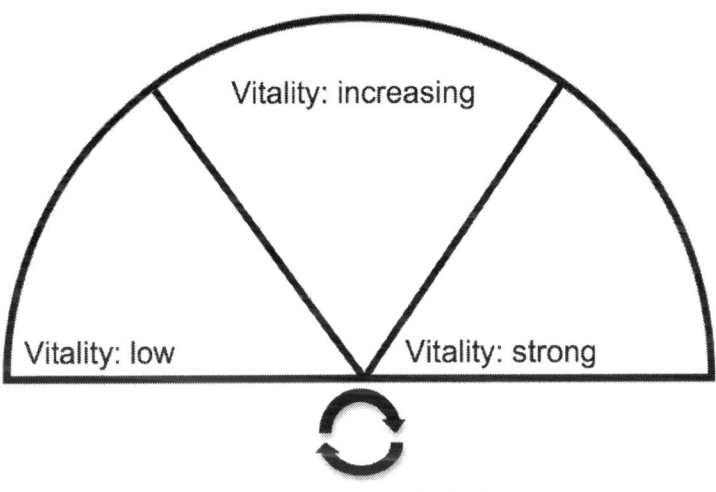

The pendulum command is:

"Increase the vitality to 1000%" (I know this is not a real number, you just want to create an excess of vitality for the person to use.)

Step 6: Check the radiesthetic color.

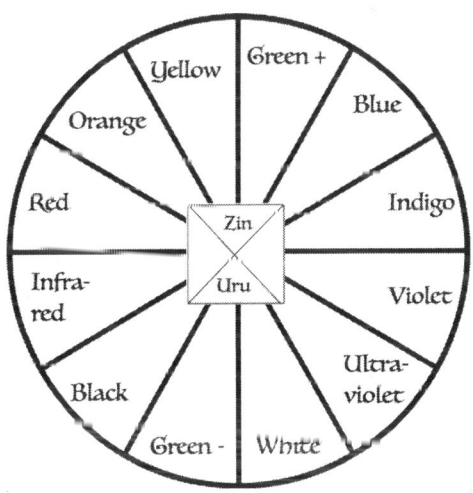

Command your pendulum:

"Change the radiesthetic color of (the person/body part) to Blue!"

(Blue is optimal health)

Note that after the healing the person may not be at Blue, or they may be at Blue, but then a short time later it may have changed again. In that case just repeat the healing. The body will use up the energy, so sometimes it needs an extra boost.

Step 7: Make your own commands

Now you take the positive statements from the interview and make your own commands relative to the situation.

Possible command prompts include:

Increase or Decrease

Add or Remove

Change or Transform

Please note that if you decrease, or remove you must add something back in after you do that command. So for example, if you use your pendulum to decrease the negative thought forms of a person, you then must increase the positive thought forms to fill the void. Use your creativity in this part, and also use the information you gathered during the interview.

Using the example of the burned finger.

Commands:

"Remove excess heat"

"Add in cooling"

Pendulum Healing

"Decrease the effects of heat on the finger"

"Increase the health of the finger's skin cells"

"Change/Transform the burned skin into healthy skin"

Step 8: Perform any other type of healing you think is appropriate.

In this step you can do other forms of healing you may be familiar with. This could include energy healing, crystal healing, prayer healing, acupuncture, massage, or any other healing modality you feel would help the person to improve. By doing it at this stage the person is more receptive to your healing efforts, because the pendulum has created favorable circumstances for healing to occur. Pendulum healing can be combined with mainstream medical care also and it can be done both before and after medical procedures.

Step 9: Close with the Stages of Healing.

The Stages of Healing helps the person to integrate everything that happened up to this point.

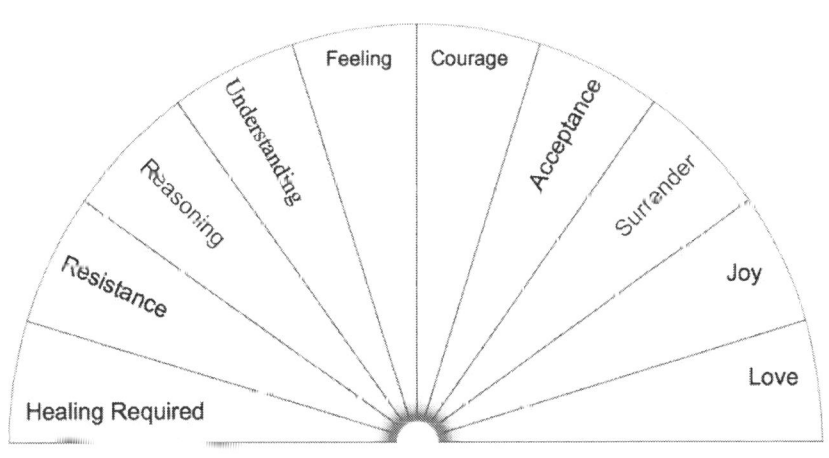

| Stage of healing chart. Erich Hunter Ph.D.

Command your pendulum:

"Bring this person/body part through the stages of healing to get to love!"

Let your pendulum spin around and then balance out. Don't worry if you dowse it and the person doesn't get to love. The act of doing this will help the person process the healing that just occurred, and allow them to move forward if they were stuck on a healing stage.

You can now give thanks as you close the healing.

Step 10: Write a healing report

In this step, you write a report to briefly explain to the person what healing you have performed, how many more sessions they require, and any extra information that might help them. You can suggest steps they can take towards self-healing (e.g. prayer, mantra, pendulum work, etc.), or point them towards other healing modalities that may help (e.g. massage, acupuncture, dietary changes, another healer, etc.). Be careful to only suggest, and not prescribe. You role is to guide people to investigate things for themselves, and to consult with their medical doctor before making any changes, or following any of your suggestions. Don't be upset if your suggestions are ignored. It is up to the person to either follow them, or not.

To learn how to write the healing report see chapter "How To Write A Healing Report"

"Quick Relief" Healing Example

In an emergency, you may need to provide quick pain relief. Here is a common example that deviates slightly from the normal healing protocol.

Example #1.

A person gets a minor burn from the stove and asks for you to help them.

1. Quickly pray to the Divine and surrender the outcome to Divine will.
2. Hold the pendulum over the burned area and ask the pendulum to:

    "Remove any excess heat" – wait for balance.

    "Send cooling to the burn"- wait for balance.

    "Bring the vitality level of the skin to 1000%" – wait for balance.

    "Increase the will of the skin to live to the highest level"- wait for balance.

    "Change the radiesthetic color to Blue"- wait for balance.

3. The person should indicate they feel relief, fairly quickly. If not, either continue, or treat the burn, with more traditional methods. Have them go to doctor if needed.
4. Silently give thanks for the healing.

5. Monitor the burn over the next few days, to make sure it is healing. Do some additional pendulum work (either in person, or remotely) if required. Since it is not a urgent situation at this point spend more time with it going over the whole protocol.

What If The Readings Don't Change After A Healing?

After you have completed a healing you might decide to check the levels of vitality, will to live, radiesthetic color, stage of healing etc. They should be significantly improved compared to where they were when you first started. If the levels have not changed, or if they appear worse than before, don't worry. There are several things you can do to correct this.

1) You can wait a few minutes and check again. Sometimes it takes time for the levels to rise. If you wait a few minutes you can get a different reading. So just give the healing a few minutes to settle in.

2) You need to do more healing work. Either the body took in all the energy rapidly, or something else has come up for healing. See if your intuition tells you if you need to do any additional healing work, or check your dowsing chart, or ask the person how they are feeling, or if anything has come up for them that may require healing. Sometimes when you think you are finished you need to provide more healing.

Usually, these actions will result in improvement of the readings. When something is off, don't assume you made a mistake, or did a bad job. Assume that there is more to be done and that it is a fun puzzle you are trying to solve to help the person get better.

One other thing to note is that even though a person's readings will be improved at the end of a healing, they may not feel better immediately. This is because it sometimes takes a while for the healing to "settle in" and/or they may require more healings. If you sense that a person requires more healing work, let them know. You can dowse how many more sessions they will require until what you can do to help is complete.

Healers Ethics

When doing healing, I suggest you follow a code of ethics. It helps you to keep your healing work positive, and ensures that you will get the best outcomes in each situation you are working on.

Here are my suggested guidelines:

Offer your healing out of love, and for the highest good of the person, yourself and all concerned.

Many healers make the mistake of failing to do this. As a result they get sick from doing a healing, or they try to force their will on others. By making this affirmation at the start, you can be assured that your healing work will not drain you. Also, what you do will only effect the person in positive ways if it is for their highest good. This also gives you free pass to do healings for people even if they can't agree to it (e.g. someone in the hospital) because it is an act of love.

Let go of any attachment to outcome. The ego wants results. You are called to play a role. Do your best and then let go.

I have found that becoming identified with the results of my healing work is the surest way to negate the effects. It is great when someone tells us what we did really helped them, but it is the negative part of the ego that wants results. I have found that we can effect healing in many ways. Some of them are obvious, some of them are subtle. Healing can be physical, mental, emotional, and spiritual. You will never know how your healing work will affect someone in a positive way. So just trust the process and believe that whatever actions you take are the right ones, regardless of results.

Only use your powers for good, no matter how tempting or justified you feel to hurt someone.

Once you start doing this work, you will realize that you can affect your world. A temptation could exist to use your powers in ways that could harm others. Human beings can very easily justify violence, hatred and revenge for moral, or just reasons. I suggest that no matter how tempting, you do not go down this road. Even once even if you feel tempted, or justified. I ask that you only use this work for increasing the amount of love in the world.

Always trust yourself. Never doubt your healing efforts.

When you are doing this work, learn to trust yourself and follow your intuition. Never doubt your actions. Always trust yourself and what you decide to do during a healing. Once the healing is done, trust that your efforts are finished for the time being and that it will work if it is supposed to. The more faith you have in yourself and the more detached you become, the more effective your pendulum work will be.

How To Write A Healing Report

If you are doing a healing, it can be useful to create a healing report. This is especially true, if the person is paying you for the healing. The healing report provides information for the person you are helping. It briefly tells them what you did, and it also provides suggestions for future actions they can take to improve their health. It also provides you with a record, in case that person contacts you for a healing again. You can use this general format to help you create your own version of the healing report. Feel free to modify it for your needs.

Healing Report for: (Name of Person)

Date:

Record the persons name and contact information here. Also record the date.

Original message:

Put the exact wording of the person here. You use this to help you determine what to focus on for the healing. You also want to keep it as a record so that you will remember what the issues were that you worked on. I also use this section to reformulate the complaints of the person into positive phrases that I can then use during the healing. For example, if someone's foot is in pain, rewrite it, as "foot feels great". Once you have recorded this information, make sure to ask the person clarifying questions to be sure you understand what is going on. Many times people will know exactly what is wrong with them, and in this section you can get that information and use it for the healing. I don't claim to be psychic, or a medical doctor, so I don't diagnose anyone. I use the information they give me to do the healing. I ask questions to follow up on hunches, intuition and Divine guidance.

Observations:

Here you want to record any observations you made during the healing, and any intuitive "downloads" you may have had. By observations, I mean things you noticed about the person you are healing, or things you noticed happening during the healing. Perhaps something in the way the person spoke or acted gave you distinct impression that is related to their healing. Maybe you noticed that they have stuck energy, or energy blockages. Maybe spirit gave you a message about what to focus on. Any impressions that you have get recorded here.

Healing performed:

I like to briefly mention the work that I did. If you are doing a distance healing, the person might not have any idea how much work you put into their healing. This way they know you did something. You don't need to go into elaborate detail. Just list the protocols used and any special things that you did during the healing (e.g. standard pendulum treatment, shamanic soul retrieval, energy healing, non-denominational prayer, etc.).

Healing sessions required:

You can dowse this on a number chart, or use your intuition. Be honest here. Tell people exactly what you think. It is up to them to decide if they want to work with you again, but you can suggest how many sessions you think they need. Most healers skip this step and it is great disservice to the people they are helping. I have been to healers in the past who just did the session for me and just disappeared leaving me confused as to what I was supposed to do next. By telling the person how many sessions they need, you are giving them valuable information that they cannot determine on their own.

Extra information that may be helpful:

In this section I tell people exactly what I recommend they should do to continue their healing. I will give instructions, and suggestions. It could be anything from prayer, to dietary changes, to getting professional help from other healers etc. It is good to engage people in their own healing if they are open to it. This is the section where you tell them what is next, and what they can do. I put the disclaimer on it about seeing your doctor before trying any of my suggestions. Try to word it so that they are at choice, and avoid words such as "should" or "required". These are just suggestions, they can take it, or leave it. Keep this section optional, but informative.

Closing

Once again thank you for asking for my help.

Please feel free to contact me with any questions you may have.

Sincerely,

Erich Hunter

I always put a note at the end asking them to contact me with any questions they have. That way they feel comfortable communicating with you and it also increases the likelihood they will seek your services again since you can be reached. I make it point to answer as many questions as I can. I think that helps the people you serve.

Disclaimer

In some parts of the world you cannot legally do spiritual healing for another person. In the state of California U.S.A. where I live I can perform pendulum healing as long as I provide a disclaimer to the person I am working on that basically says I am not a medical doctor. Here is a general statement that may work for you. Check your local laws!!!!

California has the exact points required laid out in a legal document that you can find online. Here is the one I use.

There is no guarantee that Dr. Hunter's services will solve a particular condition.

I (Erich Hunter) disclose to the client(s) in this written statement using plain language the following information:

- (A) I am not a licensed physician.
- (B) That the treatment is alternative or complementary to healing arts services licensed by the state of California, USA.
- (C) That the services to be provided are not licensed by the state.
- (D) The nature of the services to be provided are based on spiritual and energetic healing.
- (E) The theory of treatment upon which the services are based: spiritual healing, energy healing.
- (F) My educational, training, experience, and other qualifications regarding the services to be provided: Self-study, spiritual guidance.

Seek assistance from licensed medical professionals for all health issues.

Wealth: Creating Abundance And Prosperity

What is your definition of wealth, or abundance, or prosperity? Does it only include money? While this section is going to focus on finances, I want you to ponder the following story before thinking money is the answer to your problems.

I was once helping a very wealthy man. He was a high level executive in a major bank, had several mansions in different parts of the country, a winery, and a fleet of expensive sports cars and vintage cars. In fact he told me that every time he felt depressed he would buy himself a new car and that he had garages full of them. You would think this man had it all, yet he lived a life of desperation. He didn't love his wife anymore, and had almost no relationship with his children. He wanted to quit his job and run his winery, but he feared he would not be able to support himself financially because his spending habits had created a "house of cards" scenario were any loss of income would cause him to experience a financial collapse. Somehow he still managed to buy new cars since that was the only thing he lived for at this point. He also had a bad heart and he told me that his job was killing him, but that if he reduced his hours, or took time off, his coworkers would "smell blood" and overthrow him. He said that originally he wanted to be a writer, but that he was good at making money so he went into finance. Anyway the point of all this is to realize that money doesn't bring happiness. It is really your attitude towards life that will make you happy, whether you have wealth or not.

With that said, increasing your ability to receive is one way to increase the amount of wealth you have in your life. It makes sense because in order to have wealth, one has to be able to receive to get it. If you are interested in healing, chances are that you give a lot to others, but are reluctant to receive. There is often an imbalance.

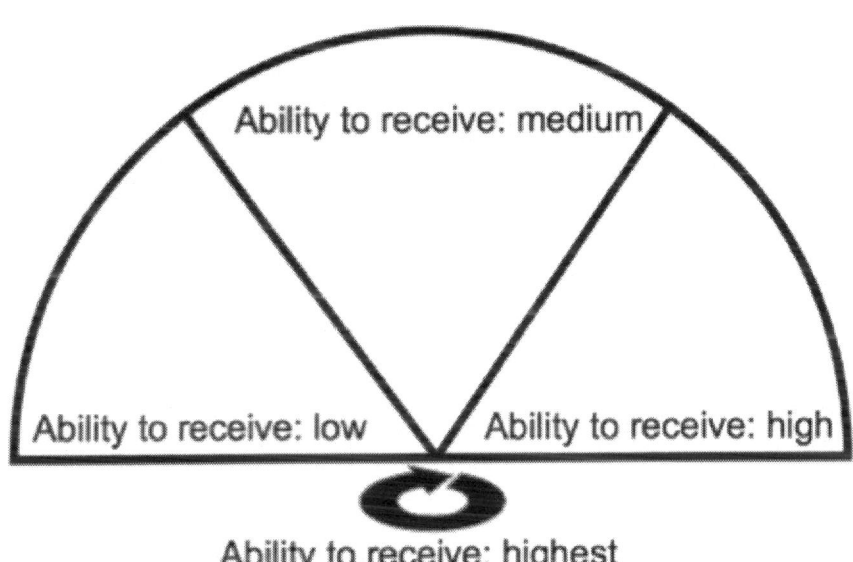

Ability to receive: medium

Ability to receive: low

Ability to receive: high

Ability to receive: highest

Use the following pendulum commands to help you rectify that imbalance. You can measure your ability to receive before doing these commands, but don't write it down, or it may be harder to change. Also, to make the pendulum commands more effective you can hold your pendulum over a tetractys if you are doing self-healing work.

This pattern of dots was a central part of the Pythagorean mystery school and influenced later Cabalists. It symbolizes the four elements, the organization of space into dimensions and has a pleasing energy so it will give you support while doing a self-healing.

●
● ●
● ● ●
● ● ● ●

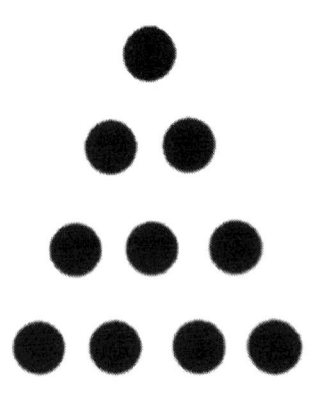

> Hold your pendulum over the Tetractys and say a positive statement to begin healing.

Here are the commands:

"Increase my ability to receive to the highest level."

"Increase my ability to receive financial abundance to the highest level."

"Change me into one who can receive, under Grace in perfect ways."

If you are successful, your pendulum will spin around in circles if you hold it over the ability to receive chart. This indicates you have given an excess of energy to draw from over time, as the work you just did takes effect.

Being able to receive is key, because most people limit themselves to working, or doing something to get financial wealth. A lot of people think they have to "work hard for their money", or that life is struggle, but to some extent, that is an attitude that one can adopt and it doesn't necessarily reflect reality. What if you were to open yourself to receiving instead? So rather than working "hard for your money", a better thought is that you are receiving money effortlessly and easily, not earning it by hard work. I have adopted this attitude and money just comes to me, in large amounts, in various ways. At times, even I am surprised at how it happens, but I have opened myself to receiving so it just comes. This doesn't mean you don't make efforts; you just allow abundance to come in and don't block it with preconceived notions as to how it should happen.

Pendulum commands:

"I am one who can easily receive lots of money under Grace in perfect ways."

"Money always comes easily to me when I need it, the Divine is my supply" "I always receive lots of money, easily."

Find ways to increase your ability to receive in daily life. Next time someone offers something, accept it Gracefully to practice receiving.

Now I want you to measure your vitality level. Take a reading with your pendulum and make a mental note of it.

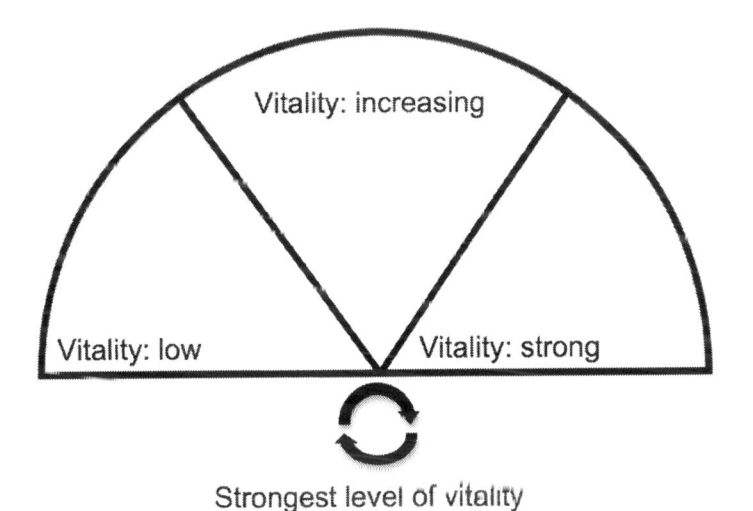

Vitality: increasing

Vitality: low

Vitality: strong

Strongest level of vitality

Pendulum command:

What is my vitality level?

Now we are going to use this information to demonstrate the power of limiting beliefs. Can you receive financial abundance if your beliefs about wealth, abundance, and prosperity limit you? For example, if you think wealthy people are greedy, would you want to become wealthy?

I want you now to think of one limiting belief you have about money, wealth, or abundance. Now say the limiting belief, and measure your vitality again. Did your vitality increase, or decrease after saying the limiting belief?

Now we are going to transform your limiting beliefs using the pendulum.

Step 1) Take your limiting belief and transform it into one that is empowering. If you are not sure about it, dowse your vitality before and after saying it. If your vitality increases after you reword it, your new belief is good one to use.

Example:

Limiting belief: **"I can't make a lot of money"**

Revised: **"Transform me into one who can make a lot of money under Grace in perfect ways."**

Now it is your turn. Identify as many limiting beliefs as you have and transform them into positive beliefs that will empower you.

List your new positive beliefs here and then hold your pendulum over the tetractys and say your new belief until the pendulum stops spinning and balances out.

Chakra Healing For Abundance

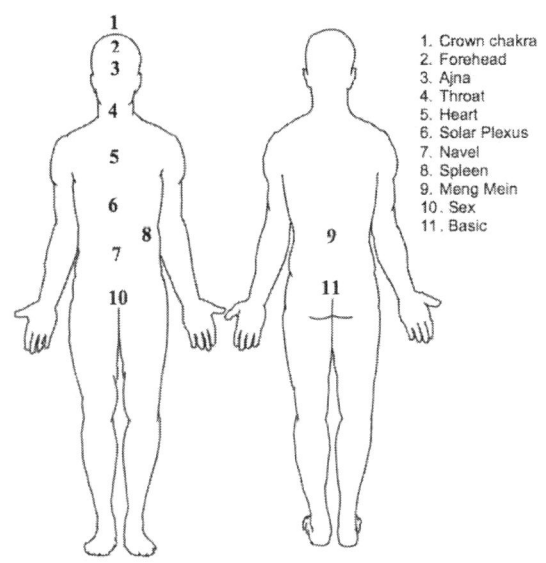

```
 1. Crown chakra
 2. Forehead
 3. Ajna
 4. Throat
 5. Heart
 6. Solar Plexus
 7. Navel
 8. Spleen
 9. Meng Mein
10. Sex
11. Basic
```

The chakra as presented by Master Choa Kok Sui is the system adopted by the author. This esoteric system is more complete than the traditional seven-chakra system that is popular with the general public.

The health of your chakra system can affect the amount of abundance in your life. One obvious example is your root (basic) chakra. If this chakra is not strong, it will be difficult to have material abundance since this chakra grounds you to the earth and brings vital energies to the rest of your body. People who are powerful at making money have a strong root chakra.

To heal your chakras:

1. Take your pendulum and imagine your chakras, and then hold your pendulum over the tetractys. If you are doing it for a person, hold the pendulum over the person's solar plexus.
2. Use the following commands one at a time. Wait for balance, and then go to next one.

- "Open all the chakras."
- "Remove all blocks of the chakras."
- "Optimize the chakras."
- "Increase the vitality of all the chakras to 1000%
- "Harmonize all chakras"

Solar Plexus

Root Chakra

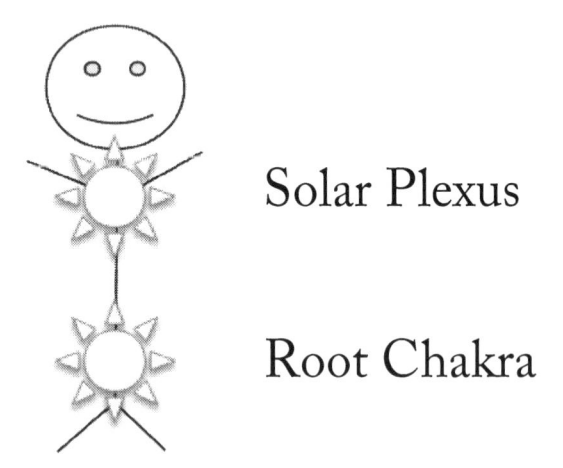

Diagram of the chakras. If doing a healing for another person, hold your pendulum over their solar plexus. If doing a self-healing, hold it in the air, or over a witness card.
You can also strengthen one chakra. Here are the commands:

"Strengthen my root chakra so that it functions optimally"

"Strengthen my root chakra under Grace in perfect ways"

Turn Spending Money Around

Lately, when I pay a bill, or go to store, give someone a financial gift, or donation to charity, I actually expect that I will receive more money (a surplus in fact) from happily spending it, or giving it away. Because of this practice, money comes to me in unexpected ways and I always have money. For example I recently got a check for $400 from my insurance company saying they decided to lower my rate and gave me a discount (I didn't ask for it, it just happened). Last time I went to the Apple Store to get a phone repaired, I ended up getting a brand new phone free and no charge whatsoever for the service (another $400 value). Whenever I sign my name on a bill, I put a happy face next to it. I basically make the act of spending money, and giving money away a joyous act and I fully expect that more money is coming and that I have a surplus of money at all times.

Now use your pendulum again and try the following commands. Feel free to modify them, or make up your own. You can hold it over the tetractys again to give it more energy.

Pendulum commands:

"Spending money makes me more money than I currently have (gets me a surplus), under Grace in perfect ways."

"The more I give, the more I receive, so I always have a surplus of money, for the highest good of all concerned."

"I happily give away money to others who I want to help, knowing that my needs are always met in abundance under Grace in perfect ways."

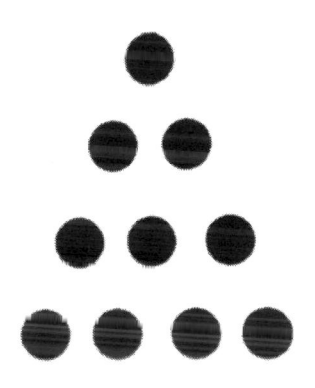

Have you ever been involved in a financial transaction that could be risky? Your pendulum can help you by creating an aura of psychic protection and by changing the consciousness of any situation you are involved in. This could be the purchase of a high priced item like a house, or a major business deal, or even something like your brokerage account. Here are the commands to use.

Pendulum commands:

"I am protected during this financial transaction. What is mine can't be lost."

"I am protected from harm under Grace in perfect ways."

"This transaction will go smoothly, and will be a win-win situation for everyone involved under Grace in perfect ways."

"What is mine by Divine right can't be lost, under Grace in perfect ways."

Receiving Money Rightfully Owed You

Are you a business owner who has to collect unpaid invoices? Are you owed money for something you sold, money you loaned, or some service you provided? Maybe you need to collect on an insurance claim, or a legal settlement. I have found the following commands to be quite effective. I have literally helped people collect thousands of dollars' worth of unpaid debt using this technique.

Pendulum commands:

"Name of Person pay me now. Send me/pay me the money you owe me for _____ now, if it is in the highest good of all concerned."

"Name of person put my check in the mail now. Pay me now, if it is in the highest good of all concerned."

Only do this if you truly believe you are rightfully owed the money and it is fair. Please be honest about this. It won't work if you are greedy, or if the money is not really yours. Also try to give an escape clause with any command you use. This is in case it would harm the person to pay you.

Protection In Court

If you ever find yourself in an unfair legal dispute, pendulum work, and spiritual protection can help. The one thing people are not prepared for in a court case is love. Therefore sending love, forgiveness, and blessings with the pendulum is very difficult to defend against, and can help you get a successful/fair outcome in court.

I recently helped a person win a court case three times on appeal. This person was hopelessly pitted against a financial powerhouse in an unfair situation. There was no way they should have won the case, yet with the assistance of the pendulum they not only won the case, but got thousands of dollars (at least 10K) of free legal help and the case was brought to the highest court in the state so that it cannot be appealed and other people in a similar situation are now benefiting from this persons legal victory, whereas before they would have unfairly lost their cases. With that said, you can try the following commands:

"I send unconditional love to all the lawyers, judges, jurors, court clerks in involved in my court case." "I bless them."

"I bless and forgive the opposing parties, completely and unconditionally."

"Divine, I ask that this case be surrendered to you for the highest outcome of all concerned."

"Show me what I need to see/know in order to take actions to free myself from any karmic debts, or bondage to others."

Use the pendulum to call for spiritual help, ask for a highest outcome for all concerned in the court case. Give up the idea of winning. Ask instead for beneficial outcome for all, and freedom from karmic debts.

In addition to pendulum work it is strongly suggested you call upon beneficial spiritual allies to protect you. I called upon a powerful god to protect the person in the court case described above and also put their witness card into a crystal chamber with the names of saints, rattlesnake and cougar images and Jesus Christ around the witness. I kept the witness in there for several months and did regular heart mediations sending the opposing parties love.

Another key point is that legal battles often involve unresolved karma, so if you find yourself in one, start trying to see what spiritual lessons you can learn from it. The more you can learn, the more likely you will be able to release the karmic bonds that are holding you back. This takes consciousness though, because often you will be angry, or hurt by the person who you are in a legal battle against, so you need to drop the whole war metaphor and approach it from a place of forgiveness and love. If you aren't willing to do this work completely and surrender the whole idea of winning, you won't be successful.

Other Ways to Increase Wealth, Abundance and Prosperity

- Cultivate gratitude. Be grateful for what you have. It will increase your ability to attract more. Use the pendulum to strengthen this.
- "Don't worship false idols" remember that the Divine is your supply, not your bank account. Call upon the Divine for assistance with increasing abundance in your life. Use your pendulum to strengthen it.
- A great way to increase abundance in your life is to help other people. I call this making deposits in the "Cosmic Karma Bank." There are many ways to do this. Find a way that brings you joy.

- Use your pendulum to ask for things. Just make sure to include "under Grace in perfect ways" at the end of your request. For example: "Divine beloved help me obtain and an abundance of _____ under Grace in perfect ways" and wait for your pendulum to stop spinning.
- If you are envious of someone use your pendulum to empower the following affirmation from Florence Scovel Shinn: "What the Divine does for others, it now does for me and more, if it is meant to be, under Grace, in perfect ways." It also helps to remember that when you are envious you don't really know what the other person's life is like. They might envy you.

Self-Expression

As healers, highly sensitive people, and empaths it is often difficult for us to express ourselves freely, since we can feel and sense when others disprove of our views. The problem is that our unique views are needed to help others, who are eager to hear us. So self-expression is of vital importance for transforming the world.

Measure your vitality (Don't write it down)

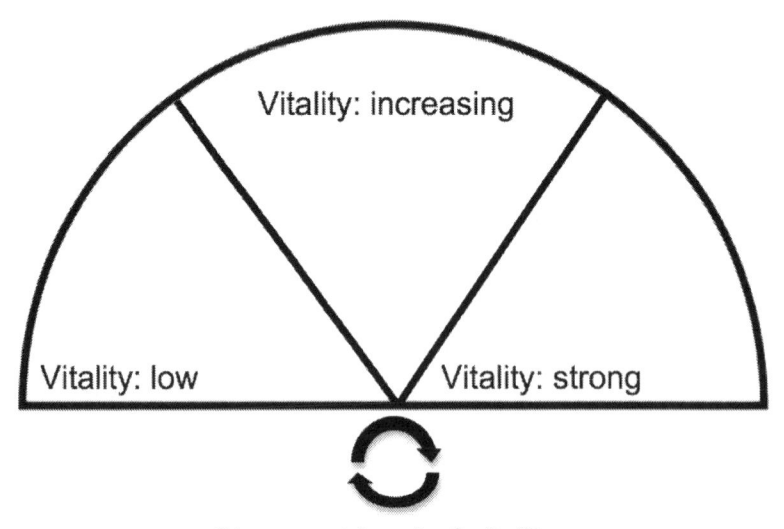

Vitality: increasing

Vitality: low   Vitality: strong

Strongest level of vitality

Now say one of the following pendulum commands:

"Change me into one who can express what I feel, and make my voice heard."

or

"I let go of the need for approval, and express myself freely."

or

"Remove any blocks I have to self-expression from this lifetime, or any other lifetime."

Measure your vitality again. Has it increased, or decreased?

If you are like most people I have encountered, your vitality will be increased. Not expressing ourselves is literally draining us of our life force vitality. There is a risk though, because expressing yourself in certain circumstances could result in injury, or even death. So we always have to balance self-expression against what is allowable by the group. This can be taken too far though, and the more you can edge towards self-expression, the healthier you will be.

The health of the chakra system is also vital for self-expression. The throat and solar plexus chakras support proper self-expression.

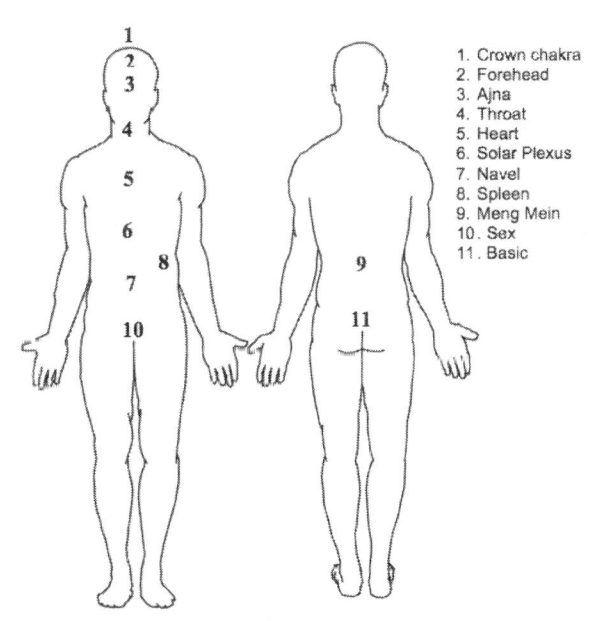

1. Crown chakra
2. Forehead
3. Ajna
4. Throat
5. Heart
6. Solar Plexus
7. Navel
8. Spleen
9. Meng Mein
10. Sex
11. Basic

The chakra as presented by Master Chua Kok Sui is the system adopted by the author. This esoteric system is more complete than the traditional seven-chakra system that is popular with the general public.

Here are some pendulum commands you can use:

"Strengthen and harmonize my throat chakra so that it functions optimally, and I can express myself."

or

"Strengthen and harmonize my solar plexus chakra so that I have the will to express myself, under Grace in perfect ways."

If you find your throat or chest tightening when you express yourself work on the solar plexus and then try the following command:

"Change me into one who can let tension pass through me."

Some people have difficulty expressing emotions due to an underdeveloped heart chakra. So you can work on that chakra as well.

Transforming Your Life Path

If you would like to change the way your life is unfolding, you can use the pendulum to support that process indirectly by energetically changing parameters that are preventing change.

Consciousness means awareness. If you are not aware of opportunities and possibilities it will be difficult to transform your life path.

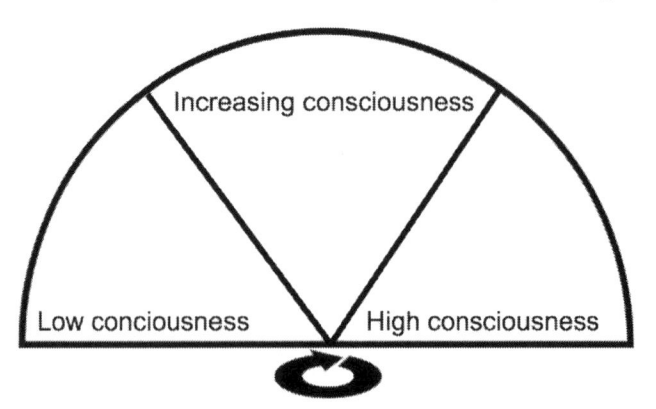

Increasing consciousness

Low conciousness   High consciousness

Highest level of consciousness

Now say the following command:

"Raise my consciousness to the highest level possible."

Be aware that increasing your consciousness means awareness of everything. Things you like and things you don't like. When you do this work, your life will change because you will be aware of things you were not aware of before. This may make you uncomfortable until you learn how to operate at this new level of awareness. So when you do transformative work you may find you are getting out of your comfort zone. You may also find that you self-sabotage yourself in order to get back into that comfort zone. Increasing your consciousness can help you to see this and to take the steps needed to evolve to the next level.

Another aspect of transforming your life path is creativity. If you aren't creative, you won't find your way around obstacles, or make opportunities for yourself to transform.

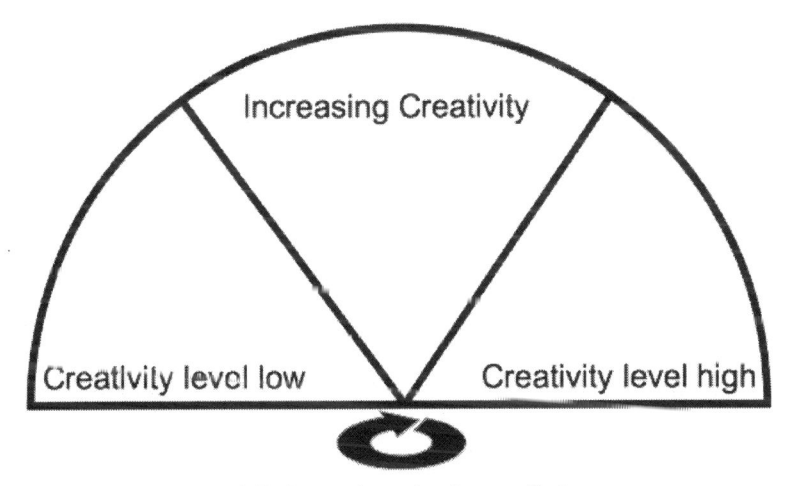

Increasing Creativity

Creativity level low | Creativity level high

Highest level of creativity

The following pendulum command can help:

"Bring my creativity to the highest level possible."

In some cases Karmic bonds and binding to other people are preventing you from going on your life path. In these cases you need to free yourself from these bonds. In the case of karma, it is essential to learn the lesson and free yourself through acceptance and forgiveness. For binding by other people in this lifetime, the bonds just need to be removed. Use the following Yes/No chart to see if Karmic influences are affecting you.

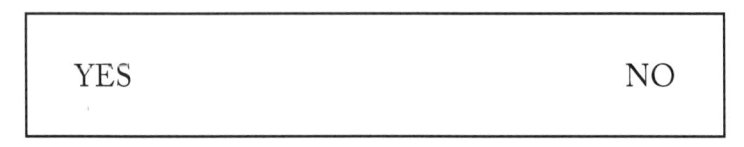

YES	NO

If yes, the following pendulum command will help:

"Help me see whatever it is I need to see, learn whatever it is I need to learn, to be free me from all karmic debts and bonds to others."

I don't believe that Karma is a form of punishment. Rather I see it as a learning opportunity to help learn life lessons so that the soul can continue its ascension. The practical implication is that when healing an issue that could be related to karma, you want to ask, **"What do I need to see?" "What lessons can be learned?" "Show me what I need to know."**

Another aspect is love and forgiveness. If you are karmic bonded to someone and it is difficult the goal here is to learn the lessons and forgive the person and bless him or her so that you can move on. Forgiving does not mean condoning bad behavior. Forgiving means that you don't hold on to it. It is a form of "surrender." Things like righteous anger will just keep you trapped and retard your personal evolution by keeping you stuck in the same cycles over and over.

The key here is that after you do this, you have to pay attention to what presents itself and then take action. This often takes courage, especially with karmic issues because it often means you have to face something that we have not learned in other lifetimes, so it may be hard to face, or we may resist. That is why it is happening. The key to solving all this is love and acceptance.

Pendulum commands:

"I send love to myself and everyone who is trying to keep me in bondage. I love accept and forgive others and myself. I am now free."

"Dear Higher Power send the highest frequencies and potencies of love to all the people on this witness card. Under Grace, in perfect ways for the highest good of all."

Put in the names of people who you think may be keeping you in bondage, or whom you might have a karmic connection with. Also put the names of people you dislike, or even hate. The pendulum should spin and then balance out. Act on the information and insights you receive.

Manifesting Ideal Work

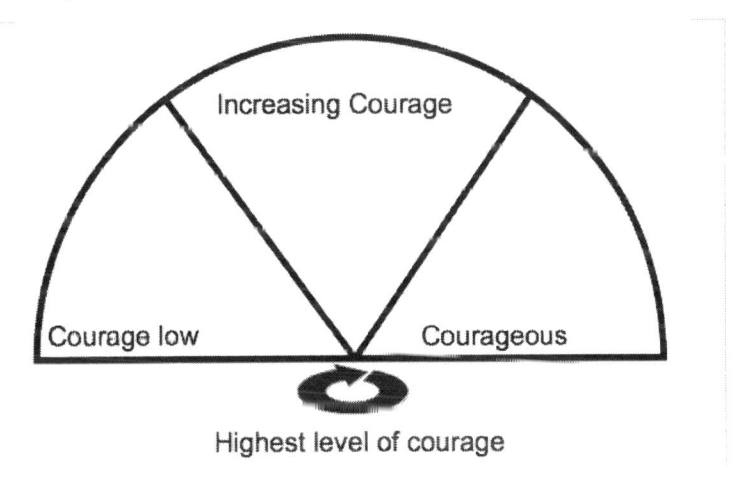

Increasing Courage

Courage low   Courageous

Highest level of courage

Courage is acting in spite of fear. To manifest your life path, it is important to be able to be in the unknown. This can be fearful and requires courage for you to move forward.

Pendulum commands:

"Dear Higher Power increase my courage to the highest level possible. Under Grace in perfect ways."

"Increase my courageousness to the highest level possible."

"Give me the courage to be true to myself, even when I am out of my comfort zone, raise me to the highest level of courage possible."

Other useful pendulum commands:

"Help me to know what my next step is on my "career path."

"Help me to know in my heart what I am meant to do" "I can follow my joy."

"Dear God show me my path."

This will not replace your need to do work, make efforts, get help, etc. It will support you however, and make your efforts more likely to succeed.

Relationship To Self: Self Love

A positive relationship with self is crucial for success in any kind of relationship. It is also vital for your health.

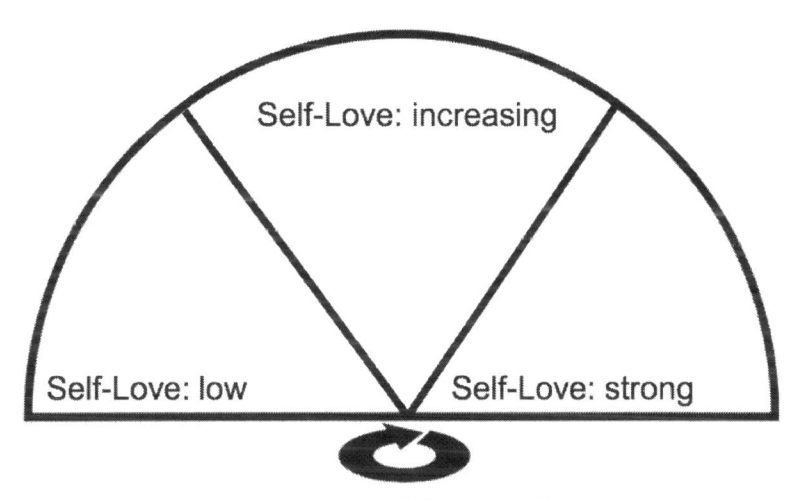

Self-Love: increasing

Self-Love: low   Self-Love: strong

I Love Myself Powerfully

Measure you level of self-love (Don't record it).

Positive statements to support self-love: Get your pendulum hold it over the Yin and Yang diagram, then say the following commands:

The Yin and Yang is a powerful harmonizing symbol. Looking at it while using your pendulum to work on relationships and it will help to provide you with harmony and balance.

"Even though (Insert a statement that makes you feel unworthy). I love, accept, and forgive myself unconditionally."

"Transform me into one who loves myself powerfully."

"Take away anything that is not self love" "Replace it with powerful self-love."

"Transform me into my own best friend."

"I love myself even if others don't love me." "Remove any blocks I have to self-love." "Fill me with self-love."

Soul Retrieval

It is believed that the "soul" can become fragmented by traumatic events and difficult situations. Common examples are child abuse, a terrible car accident or even intense encounters with another person (e.g. sexual experiences, relationships, etc.). These can cause fragmentation of the soul. Parts of the soul leave the body, and this can create various problems for a person in life. One sign of soul fragmentation is low sense of self. You can retrieve these soul fragments, however, and make yourself whole again.

Pendulum commands:

"Gather any lost soul fragments and reunite them with me now in perfect ways."

"Remove the energy of trauma and fear from the soul fragments and the auric field."

"Integrate the soul fragments so that I am now complete." "Reunite the soul with the body."

This process can be done quite effectively and quickly with a pendulum. In shamanic traditions the soul retrieval is very elaborate processes. The pendulum work, however, is less colorful, and dramatic, but it achieves the same result. I have found that you only need to do this once for a person. There is no need to repeat it, unless something traumatic was to happen to the person again.

Relations With Others

Creating harmony with others using a pendulum. Use this with any situation where people are having conflict with each other, or where you want to create the potential for good, amicable relations, while not negating free will of the parties involved. The process described below is extremely valuable and works incredibly well. I have used it to smooth out relationships between co-workers, family members, and people in the community. Use it any time to assist people who are having trouble getting along. I recommend using all the commands listed below and trying them in different permutations (e.g. Create potential for harmony between me and person x. Create potential for harmony between person x and me.)

Pendulum commands:

"Transform negative thought forms, emotions and memories between (Person) and (Person) into neutral thought forms, emotions and memories."

"Create the potential for harmony between (Person) and (Person)."

"Increase the consciousness of the situation between (Person) and (Person)."

If we can see the humanity of another person we can't hate them or hurt them. It is only when we see people as being other, or less than human, that we can be cruel. That is why helping people see each other's humanity is an important part of relationship work.

"(Person) and (Person) now see each other as human beings."

"I see the humanity in _____."

Forgiveness helps interpersonal relations. Forgiving means letting go of the insult/hurt that you are carrying. It does not mean you that you condone bad behavior. You just don't want to carry it around as a burden. I have seen many people ruin their lives by carrying around grudges all the way to the grave. In some cases it literally killed them, and ruined their lives.

Pendulum command:

"I forgive, so that I am free" "I bless (Person you dislike)."

The major spiritual practices advocate forgiveness. Use these pendulum commands to help you forgive others so you can be free. This can be extremely challenging work. Humans are hardwired to hate and not to forgive, especially when it is justified. Part of the path to enlightenment is to do this work. By forgiving others it can help you to see their humanity and bring forth the better parts of their nature.

Relationship to the Divine

The pendulum is an amplifier. It is also a way to bring thoughts to expression in the physical world. Here are some examples of how you can incorporate it into spiritual practice.

Prayer: The pendulum can be used to amplify prayers.

Affirmations: Use it to empower affirmations.

During ceremony: Use the pendulum to help you set intentions and make desired realities happen.

Mantra: Hold the pendulum while saying a mantra. Say the mantra until the pendulum stops spinning. This will increase the potency of the mantra, while decreasing the number of times you need to repeat it.

Meditation: Use the pendulum to prepare yourself for meditation.

Given the diversity of ways we can have a relationship to the Divine, it would be presumptuous of me to tell you how to incorporate pendulum work into your spiritual practice. I just wanted to provide a reminder that it is possible and that it could deepen your work.

Spiritual Allies

If you do advanced pendulum work, you will encounter situations where you will need spiritual protection. The value of a spiritual ally is extremely important. If you have not done so already, find a powerful ally to help you in the spirit world. This is especially true if you are going to get involved in working to clear out negative entities. Some guidelines in finding a spiritual ally are as follows:

1) The ally should not require anything in return, other than perhaps prayer, or an occasional token offering, e.g. food. If the ally requires you to make an oath, or bind yourself in any way avoid it. A true spiritual helper wants to help those who request it purely for the sake of helping people. No strings attached. If you find yourself in a situation where you are bound by an oath, chances are the helper will trick you and cause serious problems.

2) The ally should be powerful. Archangel Michael has a big sword. Shiva (the destroyer) has a big spear and a cobra around his neck, while Durga is on a lion and has a big sword. These are just a few examples, but you get the idea. Find a spiritual ally who is both strong and benevolent. Call on this ally any time you are going to do pendulum work where protection might be required. If you are just doing standard healings this may not be needed, but if you are helping someone who is acting strange, or who tells you they are seeing spirits, or anything else out of the ordinary like that, don't directly intervene unless you have this piece figured out. You can provide them with general healing support, but do not attempt to exorcise them of the entity. This topic is

beyond the scope of this book.

Other Types/Aspects of Relationship

Children

For children use everything you learned previously. Another piece of the puzzle is helping you to see your child clearly and not put your projections on them.

Pendulum command:

"Transform me into one who sees the Divine in my child."

Use the pendulum commands on Relations With Others to protect children in school from bullies and improve relations with teachers.

Use pendulum commands about Relations, and Self Love when teenagers are acting out.

Here is another useful command for teenagers:

"My (Teenager) feels heard. They feel like the individual they are."

If your children won't talk to you, or are upset, use the commands on Relationship With Others to make it possible to let go of old harms and have a chance at communication and peace.

"Even when I think my teenager is not listening, I will act the way I want them to behave."

Romantic Relationships

Don't use the pendulum to try and get a particular person to fall in love with you. Instead, use it to help you find the right person for you.

"I now attract the perfect person to have a romantic relationship with (e.g. dating, marriage, etc.)."

"Change me into one who expresses myself so clearly that my "light" shines like sun to attract the perfect (romantic partner)."

You can also do all the previous work on self-healing and most importantly self-love to attract the right partner. Often if you are having problems with relationships you need to harmonize relationships with your parents, especially the parent whose gender you want to attract. If you are a woman and you are having trouble in relationships with men, pendulum healing work, and other spiritual work, on harmonizing your relationship with your father will help.

Related to this, is working on harmonizing relationships among your family. Often we are called to heal our family lineage. We may be the only person in our family conscious enough to do this. So all the information in this chapter is a good starting point for that.

Projections

In psychology there is a term called projection. It is when we put our thoughts onto others without really knowing what is going on from their perspective. Every time I thought someone was doing something I didn't like for a reason, it would turn out I was completely wrong when I actually asked the person why they were doing the behavior. It was all my projection about what I thought they were doing and why. Projections will harm your relationships to others, and also make you physically ill if they make you negative. In addition to being a clear communicator, and actually asking people why they are doing something, or what they are thinking, you can use these pendulum commands to help you reduce your tendency to project onto others.

"I now see people and situations from multiple perspectives/points of view."

"Free me from projecting my thoughts onto others."

"Free me from others projections about who I am."

"Please free me from my projections about _____."

You can now heal relationships for your community and the world. Next time the news, or events get you upset take out your pendulum and start healing. Many people, myself included in the past, think that complaining and getting angry about injustices, or telling everybody how wrong the world is etc. is not going to change anything, because all it does is contribute to the problem. Instead you can use your pendulum to harmonize relationships and actually shift the energy of a situation. Now when I hear about something that gets me upset, I take out my pendulum and start doing healing work. In some cases I have seen a difference. This is a form a stealth activism and it is a chance for you to get your power back while doing something that actually make a difference instead of just complaining. The world is much more fluid than we realize. We can make a difference, and since everything is energy and we know how to work it, we can help to shift things and make a change.

Letting Go Of Attachment To Outcome

When I first started doing healing work I always wanted to know if the healing had an effect, and if the person was getting better. Sometimes this obsessed me, and I constantly worried if what I was doing was real, or if I was just imagining that the healings were working. After having several amazing successes, and my share of healings where I saw no results, I finally started to understand that my role as a healer is not to get results. My role is to show up, do my healing work with as much compassion and integrity as I can muster, while unfailingly following my intuition and spiritual guidance in every step of the healing process. That is my work. The healing is a personal affair for the person being healed and involves many factors that are out of my control.

Also, a principle of magic relative to pendulum healing is that:

"Once the magick has been performed, desire must be suppressed so that the mind has only a detached view of the desired outcome. Worrying, or fretting about the outcome will only ground the energy and weaken the effect." Encyclopedia of Wicca and Witchcraft Raven Grimassi.

This is especially true when a person is paying for a healing. When a healer accepts a donation or payment they may feel responsible for the outcome.

Although a person may think they are paying you to make them better, what they are actually paying you for is for you to create conditions that can give them a chance to heal. Your goal should be to try to relieve suffering as quickly as possible, but as the healer it is imperative that you are not identified with the results. You did your part by performing the healing, but it is not up to you if the person will heal, or not. You are creating the conditions to promote healing.

Think of it like building a scaffold to support a building that is being constructed. You are making a scaffold to support the process of healing. By changing the vitality level, radiesthetic color, emotional state, etc., it gives the person an "invisible support structure" to help them to heal. So do your part, but beyond that, the person has to make the shift, consciously and unconsciously, and it has to be in alignment with the Divine will. Also remember that healing can happen in many ways. The person may have a spiritual or emotional healing before a physical one. They could even heal something in this lifetime, but visible results will not manifest until the next lifetime. So just do your part, and trust that it is working, even if you can't see results. Have faith in your effort. Trust you are making a difference. Trust that you were called to do the healing and that it is having an effect.

Does The Pendulum Heal You?

The short answer is no. Instead the pendulum helps to create conditions that are favorable to healing. It is similar to putting a cast on a broken arm. The cast doesn't heal you, but it helps to create an environment around the arm that supports the healing process to occur.

Various occult thinkers have postulated the idea that the physical body has an invisible copy known as the subtle body, or etheric double, that is an energetic representation of the human form that serves as sort of template, or mold, that the physical body uses as a reference for growth and maintenance. Terms commonly associated with the subtle body are the aura, chakras, and a Theosophist concept known as thought forms; thoughts that are so strong they take on a life of their own and "hang out" around the subtle body of a person effecting health and well-being.

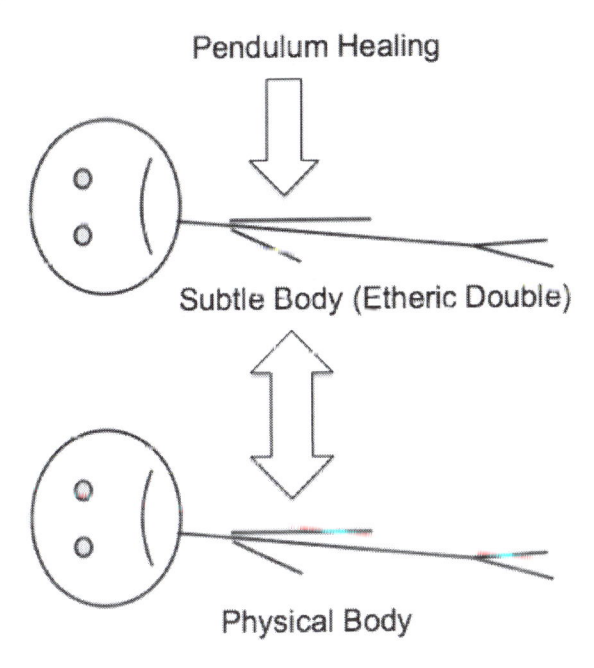

Pendulum Healing

Subtle Body (Etheric Double)

Physical Body

What pendulum healing may be doing is influencing various aspects of the subtle body, and implant thought forms in the "auric field" of the person.

Let's take radiesthetic color as an example. Depending on your state of health your body will produce a radiesthetic color of your subtle body that is detectable by pendulum dowsing. If you are healthy it will be Blue, but if you are becoming ill it will be Green-. What the pendulum healer can do is change the radiesthetic color of a person who is sick into Blue. This will stimulate the body to heal more quickly than if the body is left to heal by itself. The reason being that changing the color to Blue acts as stimulus to encourage the body to heal, because it is now "reading" the message "I am healed" from the subtle body so the healing process starts to occur.

A similar, but slightly different concept is present with the thought forms. If a person is habitually negative, or has had lots of negative thoughts directed at them from the environment, the negative thoughts will linger around their subtle body and influence the person causing them to be negative and have a negative outlook on life leading to poor health. Using the pendulum you can either remove, or transform, these negative thoughts and replace them with positive thoughts, thereby improving the person's health and well-being through an indirect feedback loop.

All of this is ultimately based on a key concept of magic (magick), namely that words have power and that they create the world (Terence Mckenna). The pendulum command, your intention and the words you use can literally alter the physical reality though this indirect process of affecting the subtle nature of reality.

Here is a more detailed attempt to try to explain what could be going on in pendulum healing work.

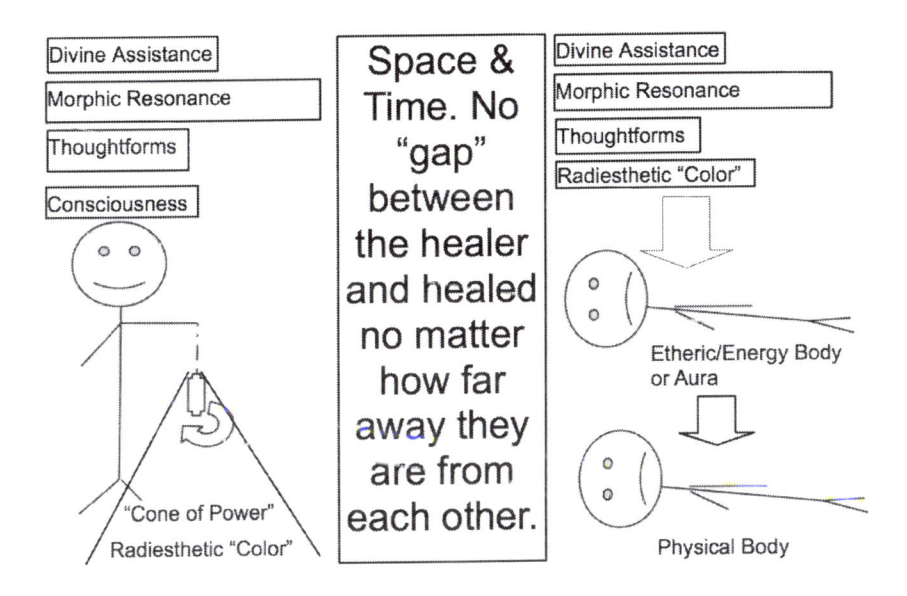

Pendulum Healing

```
[Divine Assistance]         Space &          [Divine Assistance]
[Morphic Resonance]         Time. No         [Morphic Resonance]
[Thoughtforms]               "gap"           [Thoughtforms]
[Consciousness]             between          [Radiesthetic "Color"]
                           the healer
                          and healed         Etheric/Energy Body
                           no matter         or Aura
                            how far
                           away they
                           are from          Physical Body
"Cone of Power"            each other.
Radiesthetic "Color"
```

The picture above outlines a hypothesis of what could be happening during a pendulum healing session. The healer invokes Divine assistance with prayer and connects to the ability to heal via morphic resonance (*sensu* Rupert Sheldrake) by consciously invoking the successful efforts of other healers who have done this work before, or even people who have healed from similar conditions before (that is why many healers are traditionally part of a lineage to connect them with the morphic field of that lineage). In addition, all the intentions of the healer and pendulum commands become thought forms (*sensu* Charles Leadbeater) that are transmitted to the person being healed effecting the subtle body. While the spinning action of the pendulum creates an energy "vortex" known commonly in the parlance of magic as the "cone of power". This spinning action provides energy to strengthen transmission of the thought forms, the conscious intent of the healer and the emanations of the pendulum. The emanations from the pendulum (so called radiesthetic color) are also transmitted to the subtle body of the person. Not shown on the diagram, but implicit in the whole affair is the healers consciousness. Consciousness is coherence *sensu* Richard Smoley, so it links all this healing effort together and connects the healer to the person being healed. This connection via consciousness is possible, as has been experimentally demonstrated by William Braud in numerous studies summarized in his book "Distant Mental Influence". Also there is the intangible role of Divine assistance in this whole affair. The subtle body receives these emanations and thought forms, etc. causing various transformations in the subtle body that then give the person being healed signals that health can be restored. The person may or may not be able to take advantage of these health signals from the subtle body for various reasons, and that is why not everyone will be healed.

I admit that this explanation is riding on a lot of unproven ideas. I do believe however that the summary of this explanation is correct. Namely, that somehow the pendulum healer is able to effect positive changes to the subtle body and that these changes act as a catalyst/stimulus that gives the person being helped a chance to heal. The healer cannot make the person heal, but the healer can help to create conditions that can stimulate the body to begin the healing process itself. For various reasons, however, not everyone responds equally, nor is every healer able to produce an adequate stimulus for every person, resulting in some people responding very well to treatment, while others responding only a little, some not at all.

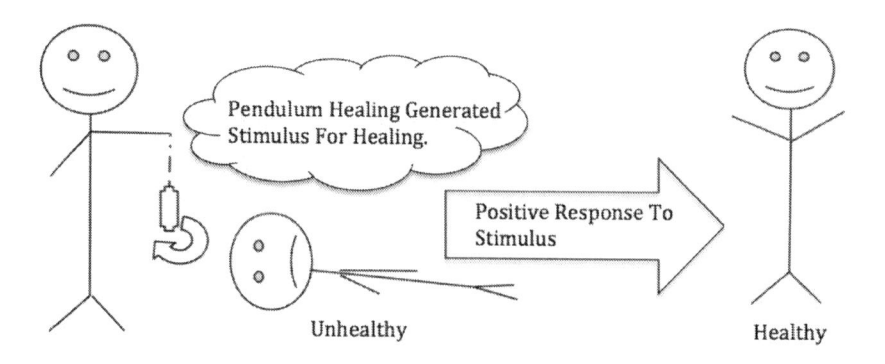

A cynic could argue it is all placebo effect, and undoubtedly placebo plays a role (Although the whole concept of placebo is unscientific, and is merely a way for materialists to dismiss out of hand phenomena they don't understand. Also, placebo plays a major role in modern medicine). Arguing against this, however, are the experimental findings of William Braud (described in a subsequent chapter) that human consciousness can cause changes to living systems in blinded experimental trials, and the fact that people (and pet animals) who have no idea they are being helped will also respond to healing efforts.

Since the healer never knows the outcome of a healing effort, it is therefore always worth trying, since it is possible to effect dramatic, positive changes in a persons health that are not predictable in advance.

Glossary

Divine Assistance: God, Gods, angels, spirit helpers, etc.

"Morphic resonance: The influence of previous structures of activity on subsequent similar structures of activity organized by morphic fields. Through morphic resonance, formative causal influences pass through or across both space and time, and these influences are assumed not to fall off with distance in space or time, but they come only from the past. The greater the degree of similarity, the greater the influence of morphic resonance. In general, morphic units closely resemble themselves in the past and are subject to self-resonance from their own past states."- Rupert Sheldrake (http://www.sheldrake.org)

A simple example is that when scientists make a new type of crystal in the laboratory, scientists in laboratories across the world can suddenly make the crystal too, even though previously it was difficult or impossible to make. The same idea is true here. Every time a person heals from a disease, it creates a morphic field of healing that can help others in the future to heal. The healer facilitates this process by using consciousness to help others tap into the morphic field of healing, and the morphic field of other successful healers from the past.

Thought forms: A concept from Theosophy that thoughts are alive and can create forms that can affect reality. Pendulum commands are the thought forms.

Cone of Power: When the pendulum spins in circle during a healing, it creates the outline of a cone shape while spinning. In magic, these circular movements are one of the ways that "power" is generated to cast the magic spell. Namely, the spinning is the source of energy that brings the spell to life, then the spoken words and consciousness of the magician sends the energized spell out into the world to affect reality.

Radiesthetic color: Emanations given off by pendulums. These emanations are invisible and therefore not true colors. The color names are only given as a memory aid.

Etheric/Energy Body and Aura: Another concept from Theosophy that has been widely accepted by the healing community. The physical body has a non-physical counterpart that affects our health and well-being.

The Science Of Pendulum Healing

No scientific/medical studies have ever been performed on pendulum healing per se. There are studies about the effect of human consciousness on living systems, however, that are directly relevant to pendulum healing and help to provide a scientific basis/justification for what we are doing.

The most prominent research on the effects of human consciousness on living systems was carried out by the late William Braud Ph.D. and his colleagues (see Distant Mental Influence: Its Contributions to Science, Healing, and Human Interactions, 2003). The findings of their copious research (and that of other scientists) are laid out in his seminal book "Distant Mental Influence" which documents how the human mind can positively effect changes on living systems in the absence of circumstances that would generate a placebo response.

Here are the issues at stake for pendulum healing.

1) Can a person influence another living person from a distance, thereby ruling out influences other than human consciousness causing the observed changes of a pendulum healing?

This is important, because pendulum healing often involves distance healing where the healer and healee are never in contact. If a person cannot induce change in a biological system from a distance, pendulum healing could not work. This is true even during an in person healing, since pendulum healing is never done via contact and the healer relies on supposed emanations of the pendulum and consciousness of intention and pendulum commands to effect change.

2) Are there scientifically unexplainable ways that information can be transferred from one person to another to cause physiological changes in living systems?

If there is evidence for this, it is vital to justifying pendulum healing. The biggest argument against pendulum healing is how can it work, since there is no scientifically justifiable mechanism, other than the so-called placebo.

Here is what Dr. Braud and his colleagues found:

"Persons are able to mentally influence remote biological systems even when those systems are isolated at distant locations and screened from all conventional informational and energetic influences. The effect appears to occur in a goal directed manner; i.e. the influencer need not understand or even be aware of the specific physical or physiological processes which bring about the desired outcome. Intentionality appears to be the key factor…" Distant Mental Influence, Pg. 103.

They were able to experimentally document that mental intention of a remote influencer could produce changes in people's activity (i.e. influence the autonomic nervous system activity of another person), mood (i.e. calm a person down from an agitated state as evidence by changes in electrical activity of the skin), protect red blood cells from osmotic stress when placed in salt solution, among other findings. These published studies demonstrate that a person can influence another living system at a distance using intention, thereby providing direct support for the notion that a pendulum healer can affect physiological change in a person they are healing through intention, and attention even when that work is done at a distance and in cases where placebo can be ruled out.

They also found that "mechanism through which this shift comes about is unclear…conventional forces of physics would appear to be adequately ruled out, since the effect survives distance and screening effects that would block or severely attenuate such forces....regardless of how the effect is mediated, its occurrence presupposes a profound interconnectedness between the influencers and the influencees..." Distant Mental Influence Pg. 104.

This also provides support for the idea that pendulum healing can effect change on living systems, even though its mechanism is not known. Consciousness and intention play a big role in pendulum healing, and the research summarized by Braud sets a precedent showing that even one element of the pendulum work (mental influence of pendulum healer on healee) is enough to cause positive changes, in spite of lacking a scientifically viable explanation for how that occurs.

This is supported by Braud's statement:

"Typically these mental influences are understood and explained in terms of biochemical and anatomical interconnections among the central nervous system, the autonomic nervous system, and the immune system...Mental processes such as attention and intention can have influences that are more direct and immediate than has been previously recognized. Direct mental influence may provide an additional control system that can function in parallel with anatomical, chemical and electrical influences within the body." Distant Mental Influence Pg. 105.

So for the skeptics and naysayers who believe you are fooling yourself doing pendulum work, they don't know what they are talking about. Published scientific research using experimentally controlled studies have found experimental support for some of main assumptions on which pendulum healing rests: namely that one person can positively influence the physiology of another; in spite of lacking a scientifically viable mechanism to explain what is occurring.

So I say carrying on your pendulum healing while the science catches up.

The Magic Of Pendulum Healing

"Magic is the art and metaphysical science of manifesting personal desires through the collection and direction of energy."

-Raven Grimassi.

Pendulum healing has all of the basic elements of magic as follows:

1. A person has a desire they wish to fulfill.

   In the context of pendulum healing the healer desires to help the healee (person being healed). The healee desires to be healed. The pendulum healer also may have their own agenda. They could want to heal relations among other people, or heal an issue in their community, or even protect themselves in a situation, or collect money owed them in a debt. The common thread here is desire to change reality in a way that benefits the healer, and the person being healed. Manly Hall, and Alice Bailey, termed any magic that was not completely selfless Black Magic. Yet I disagree, for you can desire to help someone because it would make you feel good, or because both you and the person being healed will benefit in some way from the experience, and that is certainly not evil.

2. "Energy" is gathered and sent out into the world to effect change via a ritual.

   Magic is full of rituals. In high magic they are elaborate, in low magic they are simple. The purpose of these rituals is to set intentions in motions to help the participants manifest the outcomes they desire and it is done in large part by gathering, or generating "energy" to empower the magic and give it life so that it can go out into the world and have an affect. In pendulum healing the ritual is the healing process and the steps we take to do healings. The energy we gather is from the spinning action of the pendulums, and possibly Divine assistance. The change we seek to bring about is the healing of a person or situation.

3. This ceremony takes place within a circle.

    Almost all magical traditions have the geometric shape of a circle playing a large role in the ritual process. People will stand inside a magic circle for protection, or they will create a circle by generating what is known as a "cone of power".

"Cone of power is an energy form raised within a ritual or magickal circle. Typically the energy collects into an etheric shape resembling a rounded pyramid, a somewhat cone-like image. It is often used to transmit energy that is designed to aid in healing, or to manifest a desire. There are many methods of raising a cone of power...Once a cone of power is raised, it is then released so that its magick can be transmitted. Depending on the type of magick used, the cone can be sent to a person, place, or thing through guided imagery, or the cone can be implanted directly within the astral plane for manifestation." Encyclopedia of Wicca and Witchcraft by Raven Grimassi

I was quite surprised to realize that the movement of a pendulum creates a perfect cone shape, so every time we do a pendulum healing we are creating one of the most potent means of magical transmission, a cone of power to send our healing magic out into the world.

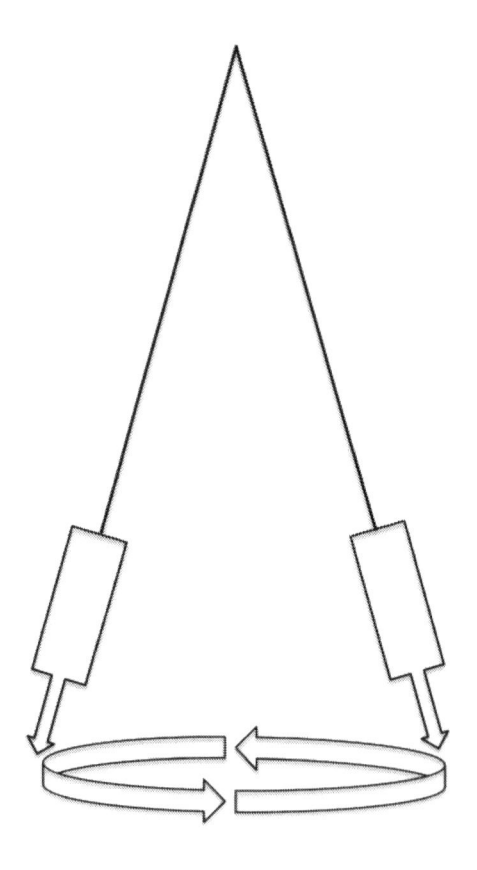

Cone of power created by the pendulum swings.

This is why the pendulum spins in circles while we say the command and then swings side to side when it is finished. The circle movements are building "energy" or "raising the cone of power", while the side-to-side movements indicate it is finished and that the cone of power has been sent off.

4) Once the ceremony is completed, the magician lets go of all desire for an outcome.

Magic won't work if you ego is invested in the outcome. This is known in circles that practice magic, and it is one of the reasons healers may do ineffective healing magic, because they are vested in the outcome so the magic loses its power.

This is one reason why it can be hard to do self-healing, or healing on friends and family members. We are invested in the outcome, so it weakens the effect. It can also make it hard when we accept payment for a healing. If we feel obligated to get a result after being paid our desire for the outcome will be too strong and thereby weaken the magic.

Notes:

1. In this work, magic is used to indicate occult esoteric practice, which is not the same as the sleight of hand and tricks also called magic.
2. An optional aspect of magic is the calling in of spiritual helpers. In Renaissance magic the magician would try to bind a spirit, or entity to them to assist with magical work. This is never done in pendulum healing, although we may invite in spiritual helpers, we never have binding oaths. Any help they provide is coming from a place of love and their choice to be involved in a healing after we invite them and we owe them nothing in return.
3. Please note, I cited a book on witchcraft because it was the only place I could find a good definition for the cone of power. It is important to note, however, that pendulum healing is not witchcraft. It does share some elements in common with it though, but these are also common to all forms of magic, and not specific to witchcraft
4. Prayer and religious ceremony are based on the principles magic. Most people who say that magic is evil are ignorant of this fact. Magic itself is not evil and adherents of all the major world religions unknowingly due magic and participate in magic rituals.

Pendulum Commands

"Magical philosophy, which has about fifty to a hundred thousand years under its belt -- as opposed to science which only goes back to the Renaissance -- has always claimed that the world is made of language. The world is a thing of words, and if you know these words, you can take it apart and put it together any old way you wish. Sanskrit, for example, has the reputation for being a magical language. There are supposedly certain ragas -- arrangements on sounds with particular rhythms -- that can cause a haystack to burst into flame. The nub of what I'm trying to get at here is that the world is made of language. Our entire Western religious tradition begins with the incredibly cryptic statement, "In the beginning was the Word and the Word was made flesh."

-Terence McKenna

A prominent part of pendulum healing work is the utterance of verbal commands to stimulate healing and broadcast intentions. Pendulum healing commands are mostly posed as imperative sentences that give a direct command (e.g. "Raise my consciousness level") and they are never posed as questions (i.e. interrogative sentences). This is one way that pendulum healing differs from dowsing, because dowsing commands are almost exclusively questions.

To understand pendulum-healing work, words, sounds and language therefore must be considered, since it is an integral part of the process. What is it about language that is so powerful? Words can control us. They can even literally kill us, as evinced by cases of medical hexing where a doctor accidently tells a healthy person they are going to die, and that person promptly does. All governments and corporations try to control us with language in the form of non-stop propaganda. People in our environment (family members, friends etc.) constantly use language to both inform us and to create security by imposing their worldview and belief system on others. We do this to ourselves in the form on nonstop mental chatter that helps us maintain sanity. A world without words is one of isolation, in which the human organism withers and dies. The question is, is it all in our heads, or is there something "out there" as well in regard to language?

Obviously, language is subjective in the sense that is a human construct, but could it be as Terence McKenna suggested, that there is more to it? That language is tapping into some primal force that shapes the world? His argument was along the lines of language being a form of communication that used sounds, which were actually attempts to create visible objects that could be "seen" to be understood. His argument was that unconsciously we use visual metaphors when describing language. I can "see what you are saying" etc. He felt we were one step away from creating a language of form, in which our words are literally objects. Are we just the shadows on the walls of Plato's cave with words being the "mold" for the shadow?

The Theosophists such as Charles Leadbeater felt that words had physical forms that could influence us and even take on a life of their own becoming a force both in our personal lives and in the collective. He called these "thought forms" and these thought forms were said to be visible to clairvoyants and to act like little organisms, genies so to speak, affecting people for either better or worse.

All magical thinking has language playing a big role, in song, story, or the utterance of phrases of power, spells, or curses. The same can be said of mantra where repetition of words is said to be able to change our reality and us. When we pray we use words to communicate with the Divine.

I hypothesize that the spoken word is more powerful than the written word vis à vis magic. A grimoire just lies there until a person reads it and then speaks its spells. Then it comes to life. Related to this is some interesting experimental research by Willam Braud on the effect of peoples' thoughts on living systems summarized in the book Distant Mental Influence (2003). He found that people were able to influence biological systems (e.g. protect red blood cells from changing salt concentrations) by their thoughts, even if they had no idea of how the physiology of the process worked. This implies to me that in healing work, and magic, it is not so much the exact words that matter, but rather the intention underlying them. The intentions can affect reality, even if you have no understanding of the mechanism by which it happens. You can get a result in the direction you want without understanding (e.g. heal someone of a stomach ache works even if you don't know how it happens). So the words are like placeholders for directing intention in some sense.

To the dismay of the materialists, skeptics and other supposed "rational" people, consciousness is proving to be an elusive concept. They claim it is all in our heads, yet they are bullishly ignoring many glaring cases of exception that strongly imply otherwise. The medical doctor John Lorber pointed out my favorite example. There are individuals who have virtually no brain to speak of due to a condition called hydrocephalus, yet they are carrying out normal lives. One of these individuals studied by Lorber even has an advanced degree in mathematics. How can this be possible if consciousness is "all in our heads" as the materialists claim? Pendulum healing is therefore at the limit of scientific explanation of human of consciousness and reality. We are acting in a realm, which science has not figured out yet.

Yes, language plays some role in all this. Finally, it is interesting to note that the use of symbols does not seem to be as powerful as words for pendulum commands. Also, written words do not seem as powerful as spoken words, although just thinking a command seems to be as effective as saying it out loud. My summary thought is that our intention is more important than the words we use, and that the words direct our consciousness so that it has some directionality to shape reality.

What To Do If You Don't Have A Pendulum

If you find yourself without a pendulum you can still do this work by using your fingers. Your finger movements will effect change, so you can use them anytime a pendulum isn't handy.

The way to do it is as follows. Take the pointer and middle finger of your dominant hand, point them towards the ground and spin them clockwise while saying a command. Just keep spinning them until you feel satisfied. There is not set time for this. If you want something to happen spin them clockwise, if you want something to be undone spin them counterclockwise.

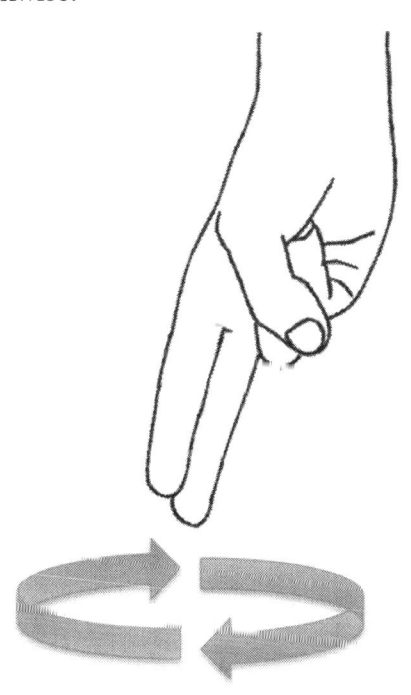

The first time I did this, I got fantastic results. My wife was going to the Apple computer store to get her IPhone repaired. It seemed like it was going to be very costly. So I used my fingers and said: "we are going to make money off getting this IPhone repaired". When they finished the repairs at the store, we tested the phone and it didn't work. I didn't doubt the magic, but spun my fingers a couple more times while saying everything works out in the highest good, and then they told us they would give us a brand new IPhone worth several hundred dollars and that they would not charge us anything for the repairs. So try using your fingers as a pendulum sometimes. It can be pretty potent, and good if you want to be discrete, or if you find yourself without a pendulum.

Stages Of Healing

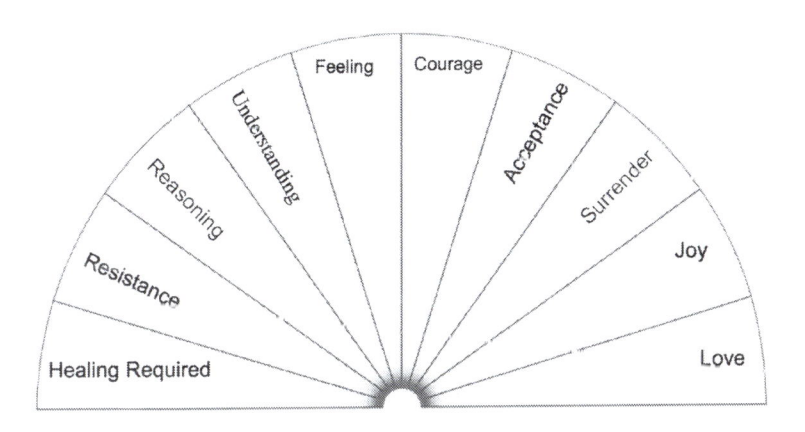

This chart outlines what I see as the stages of healing. You can use it to check a person progress during the healing process. You can also use it to encourage a person to go through the stages of healing using the pendulum.

The command to use (feel free to make your own version):

"Bring this person through the stages of healing so that they get to the stage of Love."

Wait until your pendulum stops spinning and balances out. It may take several healings to get to the stage of love.

I saw no point in documenting negative states, since witnessing things only makes them stronger, so the chart focuses on positive changes.

Some stages in the chart may make you doubt if what you are doing is working. For example, a person may have started off in the healing required stage, and then they may be in a resistant stage where they are actively (consciously, subconsciously) resisting the healing. This resistance should be seen as a positive stage because it is actually part of the healing process.

Likewise, a person might get into the feeling stage and have all sorts of emotions come up, that might seem scary, depressing, sad, etc. but this is needed. If the person doesn't feel these emotions they won't have a full healing. Take these emotions as a sign that what you are doing is working. Your task is to try to support them energetically, and let them know that it is okay if feelings come up like anger etc. and that they should do their best to feel the emotion even if is uncomfortable. If they can let the emotion play out and pass there is a better chance for getting a full healing. Use your judgment. In some cases they may need professional assistance from a therapist, or psychiatrist. Your job is just to hold space for them and provide support if they ask.

Here are some notes on each stage of the healing process:

Resistance

Resistance is often the first stage of healing. Before that point the person was probably unaware, or in denial. Resistance may be characterized by a person complaining to you of a health issue, but when you offer to help they refuse.

Reasoning

This is the stage where the person is coming to grips with the health issue and they are starting to look for solutions. They may ask you questions at this point, or come to you for help.

Understanding

The person realizes there is a problem and they are trying to understand their situation to help them look for solutions.

Feeling

The person begins to feel the emotional impact of their health situation. Feelings such as sadness, anger, rage, depression, are common in this stage. Emotional pain is often felt.

Courage

The person has felt their emotions and now have the courage to take action to try to improve their health. They are also facing any fears they have about their situation and moving forward with their life.

Acceptance

The person no longer fights the health issue. They accept their situation and don't use psychic energy to fight it.

Surrender

This is better termed as a complete relaxation of all tension. This state won't last long, but it is characterized by a sense of "weightlessness" from all burdens.

Joy

When one surrenders, it causes a complete release of tension that results in a state of joy.

Love

This is Agape love. The state of joy brings one to a realization that we are all one with each other and the Divine. Everything is beautiful and perfect in its own way. This is the highest level of enlightenment for a human.

Questions From "Circling the Square of Life" Students

Question: Can we store all of our pendulums together in one place? I have all of mine in felt bag. Will this affect them, or make it so they won't work?

Answer: Yes you can store all your pendulums in the same place. The only exception to this is the Universal Pendulum, which should be stored separately in a wooden box.

Why. Most brass and wood healing pendulums are self-cleaning, meaning that anything that attaches to them (energetically) will removed due to the constant emanation from the pendulum. Therefore storing them together is not a problem, since any influence they have on each other is short term and will be canceled quickly when they are separated for use.

Question: How do you clear a pendulum?

Answer: If you are not sure if a brass, or wooden pendulum is self-cleaning, just tap it three times (gently) on a wooden surface and it will be cleared.

A crystal pendulum may require more elaborate techniques to clear it.

Question: Is it possible that I can convince my dad, with the help of the pendulum, to go see the specialist for his health issue, or it is intruding in his personal free will (or maybe in his karma too)?

Answer: I would be very hesitant to use the pendulum to convince him of anything. What you can do instead is use the pendulum to ask "Help my dad see all his options clearly, that are in his highest good" or "Transform my dad into one who can have an open mind, if it is in his highest good". You could also increase his consciousness level.

The idea here is that we want to help people while respecting their free will and life path. So you work on something like this indirectly, altering conditions that may be preventing someone from making clear decisions, but ultimately they have to decide on their own.

Another aspect of this is that you as the healer must surrender to the outcome as well. Continue to do your part with patience and love, but don't expect an outcome and don't expect that your dad will do what you want. I know that can be hard to hear, because when we love someone we really want to help them, but at the same time it is important as a healer to let go of attachment to results. By raising your dad's consciousness level, etc. he might change his mind anyway.

Question: When you are sending a command, for example to send the radiesthetic color Blue, you're not distinguishing between sending internal or external (magnetic/electric wave) in the command. Was that to keep it simple for beginners?

What I meant to ask is this. I have an external and an internal radiesthetic color. My external color is usually Indigo and represents the electromagnetic phase. My internal color is often something like Blue or Indigo if I'm healthy (its occasionally Yellow etc. if I am poorly) and relates to my health. So my question is, when your are using commands to raise your health to Blue, you would be trying to change your internal color (magnetic phase) but you don't seem to specify that in the video, was there a reason for this approach?

Answer: I don't distinguish between those two phases magnetic and electric because they assume that pendulum emissions are waveform and I have serious doubts about that. Also, I could find no practical way to test this hypothesis save using a cone pendulum, but my experiments with that did not conclusively prove it to me. I am not saying

I am correct, it is just that at this point I haven't been convinced that pendulum emanations are waveform, so I don't recognize electric and magnetic aspects to the pendulum emanation.

Regarding your observations of internal and external colors, represented by the magnetic and electric phases of the waveform. I see it as radiesthetic Blue both inside and outside because I feel that every cell, tissue and organ is Blue when healthy.

This is not to say that you are wrong, however. It would seem like this is one of those "blind man describing the elephant" scenarios. We seem to be talking similar languages, but there are slight differences that make a difference. We are looking at different aspects of the same thing. I am not sure how you measure internal vs. external color.

What I suggest is to take what I am teaching at face value, then compare to other systems you know and modify as needed for your purpose.

If for some reason Indigo works better for you then radiesthetic Blue, it could be something unique to you. Go with that. In nature there is always a lot of variation. So my suggestion of radiesthetic color Blue is for health in general, but I guess there could be people who are not meant to be there. It could explain why certain people can't get to Blue. It is also a good reason to always add the qualifier "if it is for the highest good of the person at the end."

Question: What is the best way to ask a pendulum a question?

Answer: Using a Yes/No system seems to work best for me. Just relax, say your question and allow the pendulum to swing forward over the Yes or No on a Yes No chart like the one below:

[Yes   No]

I usually aim the pendulum towards the middle of the chart. What you should find is that as the pendulum starts to move forward it will sway towards the yes, or the no. If it doesn't do it right away, wait a second. If it doesn't do it at all, it means there is no correct answer.

I only use the pendulum to ask questions during a healing. I hardly ever use it for answering life questions, or for divination like a lot of people do. It is just how I operate.

Question: Do you use diagnosis charts?

Answer: Rarely. I don't see much purpose in diagnosing negative states. Sometimes I will take a reading before a healing and compare it to after. I don't write down the before reading though. More and more I don't bother to take a before reading and just do the healing and maybe take a reading after to see if whatever I did brought it to a high level. The only diagnosis chart I use regularly is one that shows me what I need to do next in a healing. I have all the healing modalities I know on one chart, and then I will take a reading off that chart to see how I am to proceed when I am not sure.

Question: Ideally how long should it take for the pendulum to stop spinning?

Answer: It usually doesn't take very long. Usually less than one minute. For some people, or in some cases, it might take longer. The longer it takes, the more "work" it is doing. If possible wait until it stops spinning and just goes side to side. If it is taking really long (like more than five minutes) see if you can modify the command. Sometimes that will help. Another thing you can do is stop. Wait a minute and then say the command again. Sometimes that will make it go more quickly.

Question: How can I heal myself to lose some weight? (I eat a lot of sweets, and don't seem to be able to stop it!). What orders can I give the pendulum so that I reach to the best and healthiest weight possible?

Answer: Weight gain can occur for many reasons. Some of the reasons are basic physiology (you consume more calories than you burn off with exercise) other reasons are more spiritual in nature (you gain weight to ground yourself when doing too much work on upper chakras, or you pad yourself to protect yourself from others energies). So a big part of getting to your ideal weight is determining the cause. Another thing to remember is that weight gain is not the whole story. Muscle has mass, so you can gain weight by gaining muscle, which could be a good thing. So don't just go by the scale.

Here are some commands:

"I love myself to the deepest levels possible no matter how I look or feel."

"My body is perfect as it is, I accept myself completely."

"I get to my ideal weight in ease and perfect ways."

"Transform me into one who desires healthy food."

"Allow me to feel safe without extra padding."

"Allow me to feel safe in my ideal body size."

"Transform my excess weight into energy, for vitality and health."

"Raise my bodies intelligence to the highest level possible."

"Increase my consciousness around eating and food to the highest level possible." "Reduce my stress/anxiety to the lowest level possible."

"Increase my level of internal comfort to the highest level possible."

"Change me into one who craves healthy food."

"Raise my consciousness about food choices to the highest level possible."

"Remove any blocks to me "gaining/losing" a healthy weight easily and in perfect ways."

"I can ground myself without food, or excess weight."

Remember, self-love is the most important thing. Even if you aren't your "ideal body size", please open yourself to the idea that your body is lovable as it is. Many people torture themselves because they have negative feelings about their bodies that are completely in their imagination and have nothing to do with reality. Radical self-love and acceptance are paramount in my opinion.

Question: Along the lines of giving our pendulums commands, is there a general policy regarding the number of times these commands should be repeated for best results?

Answer: There are no rules for this. I would try once a day. You could also dowse a simple number chart to see how often you can do it, or you could dowse one of the charts (e.g. vitality level) and then see if more work is needed to raise it.

Question: If blockages are due to a curse, hex, jinx, or black magic then what will be the commands to remove these blockages?

Answer: You have to use the pendulum to free you from the curse, hex, jinx, or black magic, and then you can call upon a powerful spiritual protector to assist you.

Pendulum Commands

"I send love to myself and anyone who put a curse, hex, jinx, or black magic on me."

"I love accept and forgive others and myself. I am now free."

"Free me from any curse, hex, jinx, or black magic. I am now free."

"Protect me from any curse, hex, jinx, or black magic."

Now the spiritual protection part. If you have a powerful god, or deity, or other spiritual helper who is good and will help ask them to protect you from any future curse, hex, jinx or black magic spell.

My teacher in Bali spent his life protecting people from "black magic" and he had a powerful connection to the God Shiva. What I do is once the curse, hex, or jinx is cleared; I call upon my teacher and Shiva to protect the person. Since I was initiated into his healing lineage, I can call upon them to help and they will protect. You can use any powerful God, or Angel, etc. who is willing to help.

So in summary, use the pendulum to command that the curse be lifted and then use spiritual allies and call upon them for protection.

Please note, however, that sometimes it is more complicated than this. I recently helped a man in Germany free himself from a curse he carried over from a previous lifetime. It took about two months to lift the curse. He did pendulum self-healing work under my direction; ultimately I had to channel information for him from the spirit realm to help him break the curse. Then he had to do a special ceremony using the information I gave him, and some additional information (only he knew because it related to his previous lifetime) and this involved him going deep into meditation to find the answer. Once he knew what to do I was able to guide him on how to complete the ceremony and the curse was finally lifted. This is was something unique to his situation, so sometimes if the easy approach doesn't work, you may need either go deeper and try other things, or get help from someone who has experience with this.

Question: The person I want to help with a healing will never agree to me doing any healing work on him due to his belief along the lines that only Jesus can heal, etc. However, from another training I took a long time ago the instructor suggested that we ask the consciously resistant person's true self for permission to perform a healing for the human body. The way you got yes/no responses was via muscle testing.

There were certainly clear responses to asking the person's higher self for permission to do a healing treatment for the person. What is your take on this?

Answer: Asking the higher self of a person is a great way to proceed if you are not sure if you can do a healing for someone. You can use a pendulum and a simple Yes No chart to do that. Then during your healing ask that it be in the persons highest good.

Question: I am a type 2 diabetic for 5 years now. I don't take any medication, but when it gets high like these days I take Metformin 1000mg a day. Is it possible to do something using the pendulum?

Answer: Yes the pendulum can help.

In addition to doing everything I already told you about in the healing protocol, e.g. increase ability to receive, increase will to live, etc. when you get to the end (before the stages of healing) try some of these commands:

"Reduce my blood glucose to healthy levels."

"Increase the ability of my cells to absorb glucose from my blood."

"Increase the ability of my cells to correctly respond to insulin."

"Change the radiesthetic color of my pancreas to Blue."

"Raise the vitality of my pancreas to the highest level."

"Raise my pancreas's will to live to the highest level."

"Decrease my cells resistance to insulin."

"Change the radiesthetic color of my cells to Blue."

"Increase my cells will to live."

"Purify the blood of excess glucose."

You can also make up some commands of your own for things that may be related that I missed. As strange as it sounds our bodies understand these commands and will react.

Please be sure to work closely with your doctor and monitor your blood glucose levels. One case I worked on this did not happen and as the body healed the insulin dosage became too high causing problems.

Whenever you are doing healing for someone on medication, make sure that work with a doctor to adjust the dosage as you improve, because all medicines are poisons and they can cause problems when you are healthy.

Question: Would it be more effective if I mixed pendulum healing with another healing method?

Answer: Pendulum healing can be used in conjunction with any healing method, including mainstream medicine. If you want to combine it with an alternative method such as energy healing, I recommend that you do my protocol first to open the person's ability to receive, change radiesthetic color, etc. and then before you get the last step (stages of healing) do the energy healing protocol for type 2 diabetes. That way you have prepared the ground so to speak and the energy healing can be more effective. The great thing about pendulum healing is that you can combine it with any other form of healing and it will make it more effective.

Question: Is healing the person in front of you "stronger" than doing remote healing for him/her? Or are they same?

Answer: Healing a person in front of you is not stronger. The "strength of a healing depends on the person and the situation, so it has more to do with the person being healed, than the mode of delivery (i.e. in person vs. distance healing). It is interesting to note, that some healers find that their most effective healing sessions are distance healing, but this is not universally true.

Question: Can the pendulum healer's health affect the outcome of the healing? For instance, in case of fatigue, or moderate level of illness could his ability to heal be decreased, or could he transfer his fatigue/illness to the person being healed?

Answer: In my experience, I have not found that the health of the pendulum healer affects the person being healed. This differs from other kinds of healing work (e.g. energy healing), were the state of the healer can affect the person. That is the beauty of pendulum work. There is little, or no direct transfer, or mixing of energies, between the person being healed and the healer. It is clean.

Question: How long does it take a pendulum healing to take effect?

Answer: Effects can start settling in anytime. It can happen immediately, or over the course of several hours, or even days. You will almost always notice a shift in the person, or situation, for the positive after the healing, but since it happens over time it can be subtle and hard to detect unless you are paying attention. Also when people get better they forget how they are feeling, so a lot of times you will never know so don't worry about it.

Question: Is it possible to influence someone else by using a pendulum? Would it be the same way I would do it with a spell? Or is there something else I should know to make it work the best?

Answer: The short answer is yes. I don't know what you want to do, so I ask that your intentions be good and that you use your powers for healing and helping others.

Question: I was wondering is there something I can do for someone when his or her spouse just passed away. I'm conflicted because naturally they will feel remorse so is there a way to help them go through the process easier?

Answer: There are definitely things you can do to help with the pendulum. Doing the healing protocol will help them, especially the "Stages of Healing". You can also raise the person's consciousness to the highest level possible (just use that as a command). Another one is: "Help this person see the good in every situation", or "Help this person to feel what they need to feel, see what they need to see knowing they are loved." I wouldn't interfere with a person's process, but these things are being supportive and will not stop them from grieving. It could actually help them to grieve in a healthy way. You can also ask the person how you can support them, if you feel like you want to do that.

Question: What type of pendulum is the best: bronze, silver, copper, crystal?

Answer: Bronze and wood tend to make the best pendulums. It is easiest to find a good one made from these materials. Silver, copper and crystal ones sometimes work, sometimes they don't. You might get lucky with one. You can always test the pendulum to see if it is White or Green-. Those are best radiesthetic colors for healing.

Question: If someone is unconscious, or in a coma state, can we help them?

Answer: I would do the entire regular healing protocols and add in the following:

Pendulum Commands

"Bring this person back to awareness of body and mind coordination if it is in their highest good."

"Remove any blocks to consciousness."

"Raise the consciousness of the coordination of the body mind system to the highest level possible."

"Undo the comatose state and return this person to normality."

If you know the person well, you can send them love and you can also send them messages. Just say it while spinning the pendulum.

Also the circumstances of the coma may give insights into healing steps required (e.g. was it due to trauma, undo the trauma, etc.). If due to trauma you may need to do a soul retrieval and return the soul to the body.

Question: I have an Osiris pendulum that produces negative Green, so I protect myself with aluminum foil; however, you explained that we need to unscrew the base of the pendulum to stop it from emitting Green - when not in use. Do I need to be more careful when I use the Osiris pendulum?

Answer: The Osiris is a powerful pendulum. It is safe to use. Just don't carry it in your pocket unless you unscrew it. Once it is unscrewed it cannot emit G-.

Question: I did a previous course and they gave us instructions on what you should do to start using a new pendulum. I have seen someone breathing and meditating near solar plexus, even some Reiki symbols. Do you have any suggestion? Some procedure that your energy is connected with it and also checking its color?

Answer: You don't need to do anything special. If the pendulum is self-clearing, if you try to empower them with Reiki, or meditation, it won't stay because they always clean themselves.

If you want you can make an affirmation like "This pendulum works amazingly well for healing. I always have great success when using it." That will create a positive charm for the pendulum to work, since it is a thought form around you and not actually enmeshed with the pendulum.

Question: One thing is still unclear to me. When I change the color of the person to "Blue" and try later to check where he is after the healing, and don't get "Blue" but less (like Indigo), shall I re-do the whole healing process again until he gets to Blue? (Same happened with "stage of healing"; he did not get to the stage of Love). How many times do I have to re-do it?

Answer: Yes it is normal that the person will go down over time. They are using up the "energy" you are sending. There is no set formula for how many times to do the healing. Some people just need one time, others may need almost constant help. Try bringing everything to the highest level possible. Also, the people need time to integrate. Do it once, or twice a day and let it integrate for a while before doing it again.

Question: I have been using the command you suggested to help me "See what I need to see" in order to understand my illness, and I am not sure how and where to look for the answer, maybe this is something you can help me with?"

Answer: This one is a bit of puzzler, unless you are willing to surrender to the unknown. You can't look for the answer. You ask for it and then forget about it, and let the answer come to you. I know this probably sounds like some new age woo woo, but the way it works is biblical, "Ask and you shall Receive". An answer will come. Just be aware. It could come as the form of an omen. It could come in the form of a message from a person you know, or maybe even a billboard sign, or license plate. However it comes you need to be aware and once the message is clear, act on it. Many problems are caused by us not listening to the message we are being told and then if we do hear it not acting on it. This is especially true of issues related to karma, where a lesson needs to be learned to move on.

Question: Can you change also the Radiesthetic color of your pendulum?

Answer: Unless you distort its shape with a file, or take it apart, you can only change its color temporarily. You can ask it to produce a different color and it will for a short time (while your mind controls it) but then it goes back to the base radiesthetic color if it is a self-clearing pendulum. Not every pendulum is self-clearing, but the ones you mentioned are (Isis, Karnak). If you have a pendulum that is not self-clearing and you change the color it will last for a while, but slowly change over time as it picks up other emanations from the healing work and the environment. If you aren't sure if your pendulum is self-clearing, tap your pendulum three times on wood and that will clear it.

Question: With a new pendulum I have heard it suggested blowing over it or putting it under running water to clean it. Some people even suggest charging it with solar energy, or with the moon. Have you heard about this? What is your opinion?

Answer: It is not needed with a standard healing pendulum. These procedures you mentioned are more suited to preparing crystal wands in my opinion and totally unnecessary for healing work.

Question: So is "surrender" basically just saying "whatever happens"? I'll use my pendulum for that! Easier said than done...

Answer: Surrender is hard to do consciously. It is relaxing the tension of trying to get a particular outcome. Often we have a very limited view of what is possible, and we hold onto desired outcomes to our own detriment creating a tension that makes it impossible for miracles to happen. Surrendering it going beyond just having an attitude that you don't care. It is caring, but simultaneously letting go and literally surrendering to the will of the Divine. In this state miracles can happen, in unexpected ways. It is also the gateway to the highest states of human consciousness, love, gnosis, and unity with the Divine.

Question: Which mineral, or crystal, could be recommended for a pendulum?

Answer: I don't recommend crystal pendulums. If you must have one, quartz can work. Some others will too. Unless you love crystals and must have a crystal pendulum, or if you already have a crystal pendulum, I suggest that you are better off spending your effort to get a pendulum that is likely to work consistently. Get brass or wood, proven, reliable materials.

Question: Right now we have in Northern California four major wildfires. Could we use our pendulums to change the scope of the fires for the better, maybe even contain them completely? I know it sounds far-fetched.

Answer: I think it is possible. One caveat- fires are helpful and they actually have a beneficial function in nature. I would be hesitant to try to stop the fire. Rather I would focus on protecting a house, or facility. Especially if you own a home, or a friend does, in the affected area. You could do pendulum work to protect it. This can extend to protecting other things as well. I have used the pendulum to protect my car when it was parked in an area that I was worried it might get damaged. One area I was thinking of trying, but haven't had the chance yet, it would be to protect people in war zones, or areas where bombings are occurring. Another spin off can be to use your pendulum to lower crime. I did some experiments in my neighborhood of removing negative energies from places where questionable people congregated and saw a big change in amount of hooligans and homeless drunks hanging out in the parks I worked on. The hooligans disappeared and the drunks were more friendly and polite. The whole energy changed in these areas. Unfortunately, it was temporary. A rock and roll band came to town and the energy got negative again. Some areas seem to have psychic pollution. You can clean them up with the pendulum, but then the areas get polluted again, so it is a lot of work. If your neighborhood is bad, just do it on a regular basis and you should see changes.

Question: is it possible to determine the ability, or capability of the healer using a pendulum?

Answer: Yes. You can either use a Yes No chart, or create a scale for this. It would be easy to do (e.g. a 1-10 scale with 10 being best match of you and the healer). Good idea.

Question: Can the skill, quality, or ability of the healer change over time?

Answer: The short answer is yes. A healer may do an amazing job in one particular circumstance, or with one particular person, and not have the same success in other circumstances, or with other people.

Question: When checking the radiesthetic color of a pendulum at the start of a healing, you say not to record it. Is that because our words have power?

Answer: Yes. The basic premise of pendulum healing is that our words have power and they change reality. If you record radiesthetic color at the start of a healing you stand the chance of "locking it in" and making it more difficult to change. As hard as this is for pendulum healers, I highly recommend that you move away from diagnosis as much as possible and only use it to help you progress in a healing. It is our ego that wants to see change, and also our negative curiosity that wants to know what is wrong with people. When you know there is an issue, it is better to just go straight into the healing work and skip as much of the diagnosis as you can without compromising your work.

Question: Does radiesthetic color matter for a dowsing pendulum?

Answer: Not that I am aware of, but pendulums that emanate radiesthetic colors White and Green- are also great for dowsing.

Question: Can I use separate pendulums for dowsing and healing?

Answer: Yes you can use separate pendulums. I have one pendulum that I do most of the Yes No work with, and others that I use only for healing. For some reason I am more comfortable with one pendulum for Yes No dowsing and use others for healing. So it is fine to have separate pendulums for separate purposes.

Question: Why you don't you use the Bovis Biometer? Are there some areas you don't work?

Answer: I explored the Bovis biometer, but it just doesn't feel right to me. There is nothing wrong with it; it is just not for me. Please use it in your work. See if you can incorporate what I am teaching you into the Bovis work. It is important to realize that what I am teaching you here is a foundation that you can take in a million different directions. Take what works for you and leave the rest.

Question: I noticed that the structure of your commands is based on two distinct methods. One is more like an affirmation, and the other like a command, e.g. "Increase my ability to receive to the highest level" is a command and "I always receive lots of money easily" is an affirmation.

Now you could have used the command in both ways or also the affirmation in both ways for example, "Transform me into someone who receives lots of money". I'm curious as to using either method, was there a reason you make some an affirmation type statement instead of a command-structured statement?

Answer: Very observant. Other than limitations to my imagination, I mix affirmation with command for several reasons. One, I want everyone to realize there is no right way to do this work. I have found guidelines, ideas that work for me so I share them but I want everyone to not get stuck on a formula. Try to come up with your own statements to use with the pendulum. The other reason is that in different circumstances different verbal cues seem to have more power. I base it on my intuition and experience. It may differ for different people, so that is why I try to provide several commands for each situation I address so that people can pick and choose. Let me know if you have more questions.

Question: I came up with an idea. Can the command be written in a small piece of paper and put in the chamber of the pendulum?

Answer: They call writing "Spell-ing" for a reason. With that said, a book of magic just sitting on the shelf can't do much. It takes a person's speech and actions to bring the spells to life. The same is true of pendulum work. Written commands have less power than the spoken word.

Question: When working on one's self via placing our name on a 3x5 witness card, do we refer to ourselves in the 1st, or 3rd person, or does it matter?

Answer: It doesn't matter. Some people don't even need the witness card to connect with themselves. You can just hold the pendulum in the air, although I generally recommend the witness unless you feel confident doing this.

Question: In the last session you talked briefly about balancing all of the chakras at once, instead of tediously balancing them one at a time. Of course balancing them simultaneously is the way to go. You said to hold the pendulum over the subject's solar plexus to do the all at once balancing. What if I am the subject? How to I hold the pendulum over my solar plexus?

Answer: You can hold it over your palm, or over a card, or in the air if you can connect with yourself.

Question: The tree in my front lawn is dropping leaves and dying. Is there anything I can do with the pendulum to help it?

Answer: When trees are healthy they are Green+. You could check its radiesthetic color and bring it Green+ if needed.

Question: I was wondering, if you are healing someone who is sitting in front of you, could it be done simply by looking and focusing on him or her instead of a witness card?

Answer: Yes, but I normally hold the pendulum over the solar plexus, or the part of the body you are healing.

Question: Okay, as I understand it, the intelligence the pendulum taps into can only respond accurately to questions regarding what is NOW, not what WILL or MAY BE LATER, correct?

Answer: I generally don't use the pendulum to answer questions. What I do instead is use it to try and shift or alter the reality of situation, while simultaneously surrendering the outcome to the Divine in case my desires are not in my highest good/part of the Divine plan.

Question: how do you see the difference between using pendulum commands e.g. remove negative blocks, and the radionics codes to do such?

Answer: I found the radionics codes to be much less effective. I created my own DeLaWarr radionics machine and while it was a lot of fun to build and to use it just didn't give powerful results. It seemed to sort of effect things, but not in a dramatic way. I actually found that "paper" radionics machines were more effective than real physical ones. One other thing is that the radionics codes got excessively complicated. The diagnosis procedure was too involved. It seemed to be based off a medical model, rather than a metaphysical model. Most of the radionics practitioners were obsessed with getting accepted into the mainstream medicine to their own demise. Anyway, that was my experience. Perhaps others can have greater success with these devices. I am still intrigued by them (A nonsensical machine that effects reality). If this work inspires you try using the codes, or what they stand for, for pendulum work. It would be an interesting experiment. Just note, the pendulum commands have the power of spoken word, language, and it morphogenetic field/thought forms while, the radionics codes are more abstract and have a weaker morphogenetic field/thought forms because fewer people use them.

Question: I heard that Universal Pendulums are for advanced healing work. Do you agree?

Answer: With the exception of a simplified universal pendulum, I have found that they are really not needed in advanced healing work. I had two, but I sold one of them because I never used it. I could do everything with a simplified universal pendulum and an Isis pendulum, or similar. The simplified universal pendulum is useful, however. This pendulum is a ball with colored marks on the string. You use it to provide energies needed for the health of a person's chakras. I am designing a pendulum that has a simplified universal pendulum built into an Osiris type pendulum.

Question: How would we work with children who are bullied because of something they lack, or because they are overweight?

Answer: Just use the protocol from the chapter about Relationship To Others. If possible, find out the names of the people who are bullying the child and harmonize the relationships. If you can't just use a substitute (e.g. all the students bullying my child)

You can also work on the self-love of the child.

Just follow all the steps in this book and use the same commands.

Finally, if you are open to it, call upon spiritual protection to help. Find a god, or angel who is a "badass" and also on the side of good. Ask them to protect your child. The Archangel Michael would be a good one for this.

Question: Could you please elaborate on how to develop the Divine feminine/masculine to help find a life partner?

Answer: You may have either the masculine, or feminine aspect of your psyche and spirit to be more developed. You can be a woman who has a very strong masculine, or a man who has a strong feminine.

So what you can do, in addition to the pendulum commands about relationships, is do a ceremony, or prayer, over a period of time to honor that part of you that is weaker. For example, you can make an altar and put images of your father and men, or a statue of man, or even a statue of a lingam, and honor the masculine that way. You could do mantra to Shiva too.

You could do the same for the feminine. A statue, or picture of Shakti, or a woman, or something that represents women, like a beautiful sari.

The idea is to connect with the spirit of the masculine or feminine and honor it and love it. Once you gain balance it can help you attract a romantic partner in your life.

Question: how long does it take for soul retrieval to happen and the parts to become integrated?

Answer: It can happen quickly. You may find that it takes more than once, but when I do it, it only takes one time.

Question: When you say that your pendulum should be negative green does it mean it should show its energy as such on the chart? If so, should I change the pendulum or ask for a clearing for it to come to Green-?

Answer: Yes a healing pendulum should show its color as being Green-. It can also be White. Both will work. Don't change the pendulum, because it will change right back to its original color after a few seconds. Ask your pendulum "What radiesthetic color are you?" If it is

Green- or White go ahead and use it. If it is not Green- or White get another pendulum.

Question: In the case of abundance issues, what if there is some kind of ancestral or genetic programming we are running that deepens the belief in lack. How would we clear that?

Answer: In addition to working on yourself, also work on the spirits of your ancestors, and your past lifetimes. You can also work on other family members. Do this the same way you would do a regular healing, but write the names of these ancestors on a witness card. All of this combined will hopefully shift things.

Question: I had a question regarding court cases from the last class. What kind of a command could we say if I am a lawyer and the opposition lawyer is extremely dominant, mean and is just about winning?

Answer: There are two approaches.

1) Do the work we covered in the chapter on Relationships to harmonize relationships with the other lawyer. Also, do work on self-love. Finally call in help from a spiritual ally to protect you during the trial, and surrender the outcome to the highest good of all concerned.

2) Use love. No one in court is prepared to defend against love. Do what I showed you today and the information from the last session before the court date. Make sure to send love to everyone including the opposing lawyer. The dominant and pushy lawyer may not change how they are acting, but I have seen in my experience with this in the past, that the whole trial will shift and the outcome will be more likely to be fair. Also, ask that you learn whatever you need to learn from the situation. It is possible that you need to learn how to be more assertive.

Question: A friend has gotten her first Pendulum. I checked it's Rad color and its White. Now she is just at the very starting stage of " show me Yes & No answer ". She called over to my house to see how to use it and any time she gave it the show me command it barely moved and it was difficult to see what direction it was moving in. So we tried the command "Show me clearly " and it was not any stronger. Does she just need more time with her pendulum? What do you suggest?

Answer: Sometimes you need to give it a little nudge to get started. It could have been the angle of her hand. If it all seems fine, make sure she is ready to do this work. If she is not ready, it won't work well. She just might need some time to be ready. Not everyone is ready to do this healing work. It takes a certain stretch of the imagination and a change in belief in what is possible.

Question: I asked about my health with my pendulum, and I was bummed to get an inaccurate result. Am I just torturing myself asking questions?

Answer: Nothing is as "dangerous as a loaded pendulum". If we want something bad enough, we can get a false answer. That is why I don't really do any diagnosis work. I only use it in the moment to answer questions related to what I am doing, since I have no vested interest in the outcome. I guess at least it went up less this time.

Question: You mentioned the possibility of using Shiva through your connection - you mentioned that he was good for protection but didn't mention if he was good for healing?

Answer: My mentor invoked him during healing, but then again he viewed things from the paradigm of Black Magic. He felt that he was always fighting black magic, hence Shiva.

I have only used him for protection. He could keep you safe while you are healing. I don't think of him as doing healing though.

Question: I always feel like a fake when I say I surrender to the higher power because I don't feel like I really have one. Will pendulum-healing work without spiritual connection?

Answer: Spirituality is not required for pendulum healing, unless you plan on doing work with possession by negative entities (e.g. demons, ghosts, etc.). If you are doing this work, I highly recommend you have spiritual allies.

Question: How do you know you really talk with your spirit guide, or higher self? I am a skeptic even about my own work.lol...

Answer: One never really "knows" in the sense that I could prove it to anyone else. I know however, for several reasons. 1) If I connect with the spirit guide/higher self and ask for guidance, I follow the guidance and it causes a change (i.e. it works). Then I know that I got the guidance from somewhere. It could all be "in my head" except that I have had many instances where the guidance said things that didn't make sense to me, but then either made perfect sense to others, or was exactly what I needed to know/do.

My suggestion is not to concern yourself too much with this issue. Self-doubt is really the only thing that can hinder your success in this work. That is why I stress that during a healing, or pendulum work, it is vital you learn to trust whatever intuition you have, or "guidance" you receive. It can come in many forms. You might hear voices, you might get psychic impressions, you might have omens, people may come up to you and say the most amazing things out of the blue, it could also just be a gut feeling, or an inner knowing. The form doesn't matter. Also, if you have a spiritual practice, over time you will probably trust a god, or angel, or spirit that you will feel is an ally. Even if you don't believe in any of this, I still think it is vital to trust your inner knowing.

Question: How do you know if a metal, or wood, pendulum is self-cleaning?

Answer: It is the shape of the pendulum and the material it is made of. Teardrop shaped, and crystal is not self clearing. If it is a brass, or wood, pendulum, is elongated, and has ring cuts on the side it will be self-clearing (e.g. an Isis pendulum).

Question: You also say, "if you know the command for a particular pendulum" say the command, or say your own command. This implies that certain pendulum have a command that goes with it. Is this correct? Please explain.

Answer: Some pendulums have specialized commands. These are in the minority though. I generally say, don't worry about this. Basically, if you get one of these pendulums, the pendulum maker will provide the commands.

Question: I feel lightheaded during pendulum work. Is this normal?

Answer: No this is not normal. It means that you are becoming ungrounded, that is too connected to spirit and not enough connection to mother earth. If you feel lightheaded, you can try several things. 1) You can use your toes to grab the ground, or you can walk on the earth with bare feet 2) you can strengthen your basic chakra using the pendulum, or doing physical exercise. Kundalini yoga is excellent for balancing your system so that you are both spiritual and grounded.

Pendulum Healing Charts

Ability To Receive

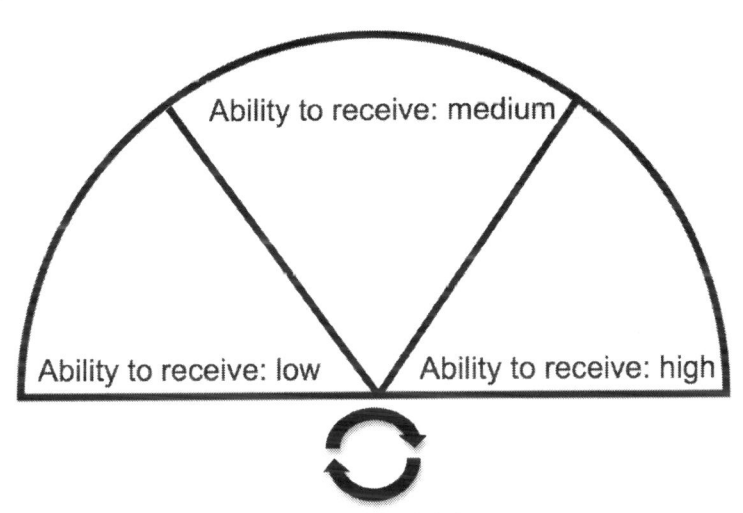

For spiritual people, the ability to receive is tied to having abundance in your life. Many spiritual people have taken vows of poverty in previous lifetimes, or have a negative attitude towards receiving, because the stronger impulse in us is to give.

When dowsing, if your pendulum spins in circles, you are at the highest level of receiving. This should be your goal at the end of the healing session. The excess energy will work to raise your overall level over time.

Pendulum commands:

What is my ability to receive?

"Raise my ability to receive to the highest levels."

Vitality

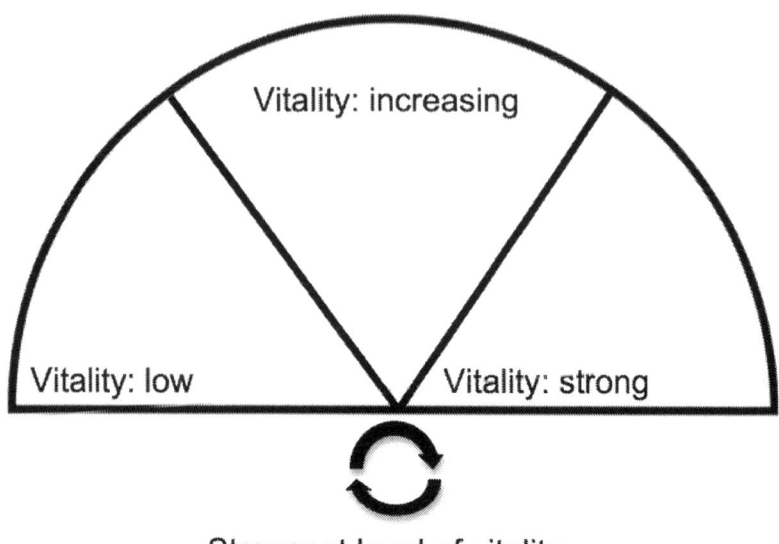

Diagram: semicircular pendulum chart with sections labeled "Vitality: low", "Vitality: increasing", "Vitality: strong", with a rotation symbol below labeled "Strongest level of vitality"

Increasing a person's vitality is an important part of healing. If your vitality is low, it is not possible to be healthy. It is not the only factor involved with health, but is good to include in any healing.

Pendulum commands:

"Change my vitality to the strongest level possible for my health and well-being."

"Transform low vitality into the strongest level of vitality."

Do this for the whole person, and any part of the body that is having issues.

Will To Live

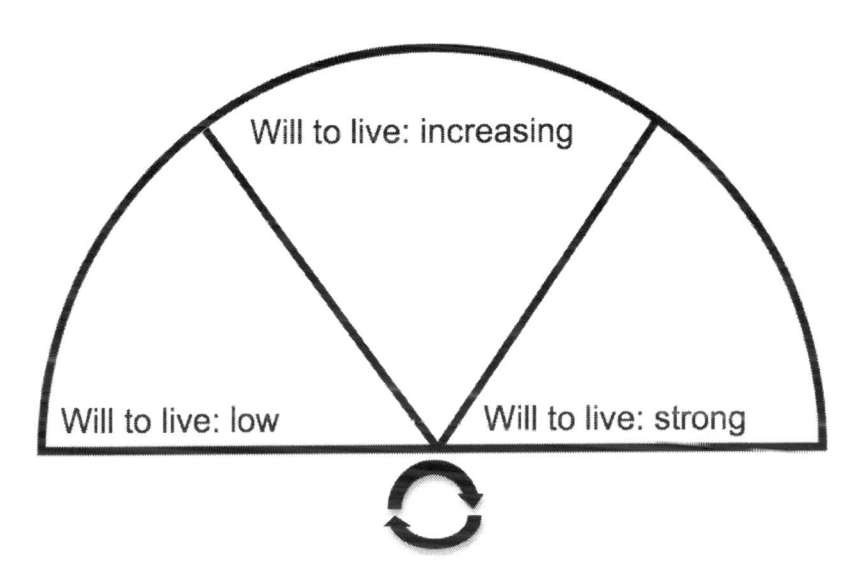

```
        Will to live: increasing
Will to live: low     Will to live: strong
        Strongest will to live
```

Check a person's will to live, and also check the will to live for any body parts having problems. This will remind the body of its desire to live and stimulate it to try and get healthy again. This is also useful for people who are suicidal and for people who are possessed by negative entities. This is related to, but slightly different than, vitality so change both when doing a healing.

Pendulum commands:

"What is my will to live?"

"What is the will to live of _____(body part)?"

"Change me so that I have the strongest will to live."

"Bring my _____ (body part) to the strongest will to live."

Courage

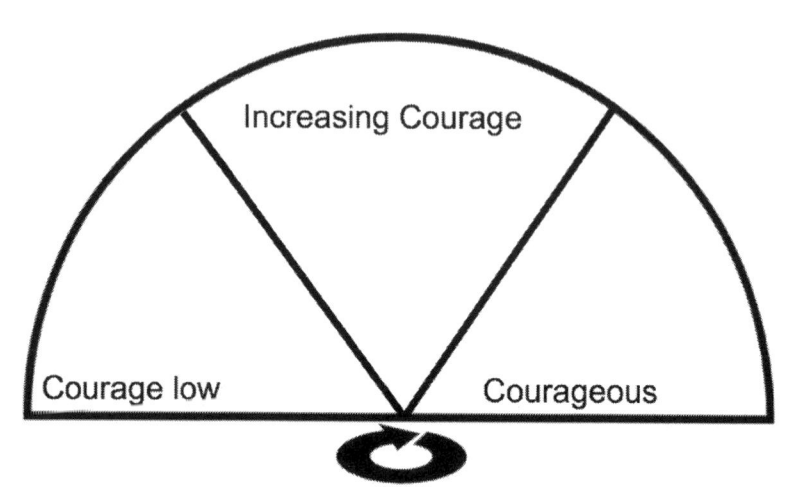

```
          Increasing Courage

Courage low              Courageous

       Highest level of courage
```

Use this chart to help increase the amount of courage you have. Courage is acting in spite of fear. To manifest your life path, it is important to be able to be in the unknown. This can be fearful and requires courage for you to move forward.

Pendulum commands:

"Dear (higher power). Increase my courage to the highest level possible. Under Grace in perfect ways."

"Increase my courageousness to the highest level possible."

"Increase the courageousness of (body part that was having trouble) to the highest level possible."

Expansion Versus Contraction

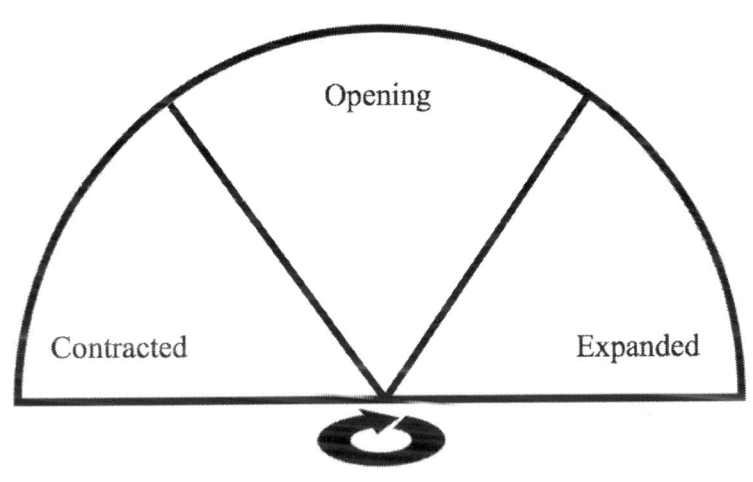

```
          Opening


Contracted            Expanded

    Maximum Expansion
```

We are contracted when tense, hateful, fearful, stressed, etc. We are expanded when we are relaxed, loving, and conscious, etc.

Measure your current state:

"What is my current state of contraction or expansion?"

"Change me to the level of maximal expansion."

Expansive states are healing. New information can come to us, new perspectives open to help us see the world differently and find solutions to our problems, or be okay with things the way they are. Vitality will also be higher in the expansive states. Enlightenment could be considered a state of maximal expansion. Meditation and forgiveness/compassion can also help to achieve this desired state.

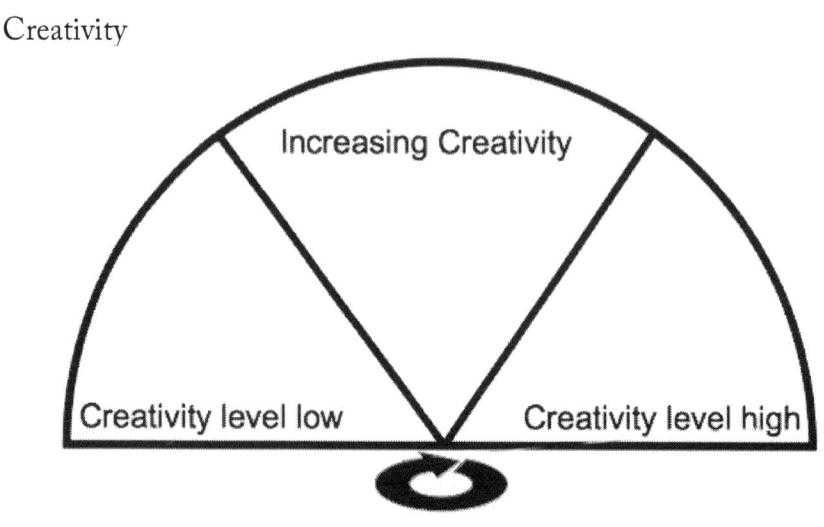

Creativity

```
         Increasing Creativity

Creativity level low    Creativity level high
         Highest level of creativity
```

One of the hallmarks of being human is creativity. We are the most creative beings in nature and that is what makes us so unique. In spite of this, many times we can become stuck in boredom, and a lack of creativity that is deadening to the spirit. Illness is often characterized by a lack of creativity as our body, mind, soul struggles to heal itself. Increasing a person's level of creativity can contribute greatly to the healing process, providing them energetic support, while increasing their bodies' ability to creatively problem solve to heal their issue.

The following commands are useful:

"Change me to one who has the highest levels of creativity for my health and well being."

"Increase my level of creativity for my highest good."

"Transform the energy of boredom into energy of creative impulse."

Self-love

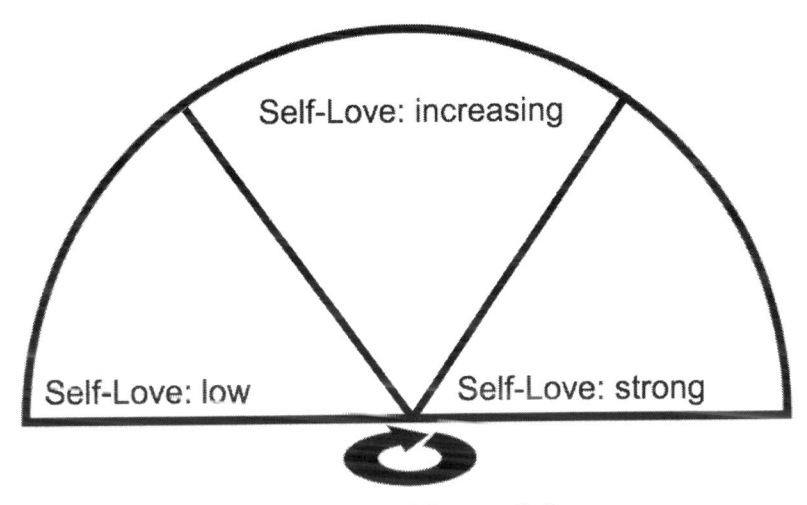

```
        Self-Love: increasing

Self-Love: low      Self-Love: strong
```

I Love Myself Powerfully

It is amazing how many people do not love themselves. I remember once when I was in a spiritual school for enlightenment and I had been involved with them for many years. We studied all aspects of consciousness and did many exercises in self-awareness. Needless to say I was quite shocked when one of the students asked me if I loved myself and quite honestly my answer was no. What a wake up call. How could I not love myself? I had been living in this body for decades. How could I not love it? I discovered that many other people also didn't love themselves and it was a source of illness. The body has no ally if you don't love it. It is alone.

To encourage self-love try the following pendulum commands:

"Transform the energy of self hatred into the energy of self-love."

"I am lovable, I am loving."

"I see that I am lovable."

"I love myself."

Loving yourself is a process. It takes time. Our natural state is self-love, so make efforts to get back to that. This could also require healing of relationships, traumas, forgiveness work, etc. Find a way to this. It is of vital importance for healing, and for enjoying life. Even taking a small step like hugging yourself, or looking in the mirror and saying I love you can be a big step. Use the pendulum commands to support you.

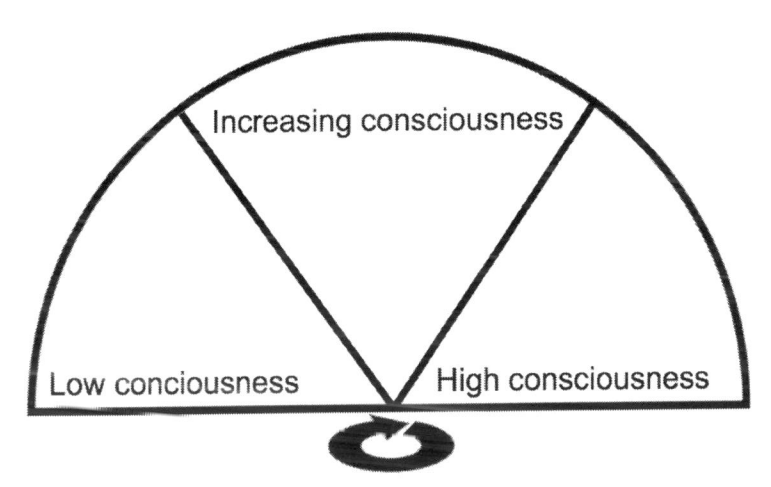

Consciousness

```
        Increasing consciousness

  Low conciousness      High consciousness
```

Highest level of consciousness

Low states of consciousness are bad for your health and well-being. Negativity, anger, jealousy, cynicism, etc. are all low. Higher states of consciousness improve health and give you the flexibility to receive and perceive more information. You have more choice because you have more options, meaning you can choose what you want, instead of making due. Increasing consciousness is a form of empowerment, but it is a double-edged sword in that you may get out of your comfort zone.

Pendulum commands:

"Transform the energy of lower levels of consciousness to the highest levels of consciousness."

"Increase the consciousness of my _____(body part) to the highest level for my health and well-being."

If you dowse yourself while meditating you will find that your consciousness levels will go extremely high. Also, if you are a channel your consciousness will be extremely high when doing channeling work.

Shame

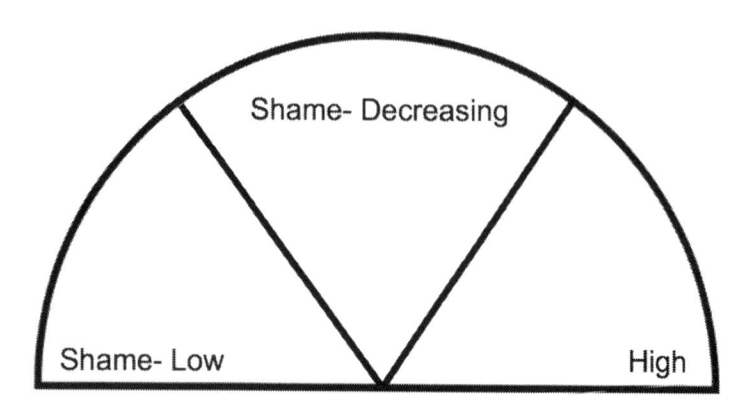

```
         Shame- Decreasing

Shame- Low                    High
```

Shame: A painful feeling of humiliation or distress caused by the consciousness of wrong, or foolish behavior. -Oxford English Dictionary.

Shame is a debilitating emotion that can prevent us from manifesting our life path. Many of us were shamed both in this lifetime, and in past lives, for our differences from others, and because of a lack of compassion by others. The goal of this healing is to reduce the strength of the thought form of shame, and increase self-esteem and self-love.

Pendulum commands:

"Transform the energy of shame into the energy of self-love."

"Decrease the intensity of shame in my emotional, physical and mental bodies."

"Neutralize the feeling of shame and transform it into self-love."

"Dear God/Higher power, I surrender these feelings of shame to you and ask that you heal me."

Note that this chart is odd in that we are attempting to decrease shame. So this chart is read backwards compared to all the other charts in this book.

Universal Healing Chart

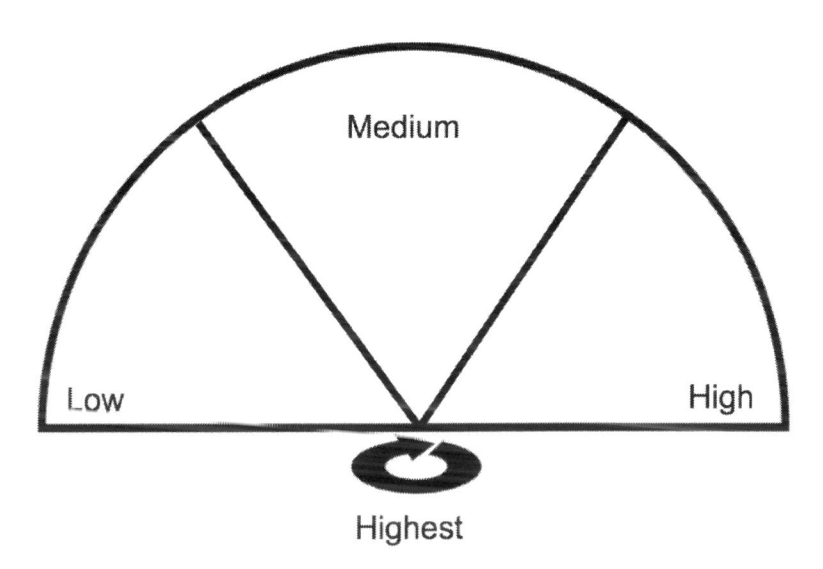

```
        Medium
   /              \
  /                \
 Low              High
       ↻
     Highest
```

Here is a template you can use for any situation. Just fill it in with a value you want to increase using the pendulum and template can be a reminder or dowsing aid.

Number line

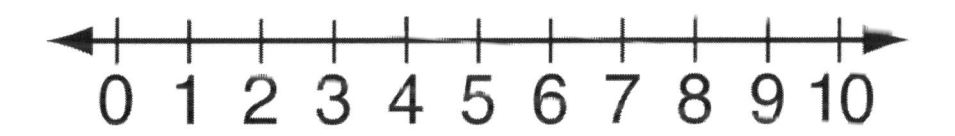

```
←—+—+—+—+—+—+—+—+—+—+—→
  0  1  2  3  4  5  6  7  8  9 10
```

Here is a number line you can use to dowse how many sessions a person needs, or the frequency of anything you need to measure. Just swing your pendulum towards the line and see what number it swings towards to get a reading.

Causes Of Illness

While I do not believe in dowsing to discover the cause of illness, I am including this list to illustrate how complex ill health can be and that there is not one single approach to improving a person's health. Studying this chart can help to make you a better healer, but it can also show the limitations of what is possible for a single healer to do. This is why we should always consider techniques alternative to pendulum healing and also seek out healing work from other healers who may have a specialty, or expertise, we are lacking. Obviously this chart is not complete, some areas are overlapping.

Causes Of Illness:

<u>Body Out Of Balance,</u>

Acidity

Deficiencies: nutrients, vitamins, etc.

Physical problems causing imbalance

Lack of exercise/too much exercise

Kundalini syndrome

Lack of sleep

Lack of sunshine

Etc.

<u>Germ Theory</u>

Bacteria

Viruses

Prions

Parasites: e.g. Worms, Protozoans, Insects

Diet

Excess alcohol

Fake foods

Excess sugar

Gluten

Genetically Modified Foods

Lack of important nutrients lack of vitamins

Lack of natural foods nutrition

Excess smoking

Starvation

Dehydration

Environmental Toxins

EMF's

Heavy metals

Toxic exposure

Poisons

Pollution

Geopathic stress

Negative thought forms fields

<u>Medical (Iatrogenic) illness, injury, death</u>

Medications

Vaccines

Medical treatments (e.g. surgery, chemo.)

<u>Inheritance</u>

Heredity/genetics

Familial patterns passed down

Miasms

<u>Past lives</u>

Karma

Residue past lives

Unresolved ancestral energies

<u>Response to trauma</u>

Injury to body

Abuse: physical, mental, or emotional

Adverse childhood experiences

Past physical trauma shock/trauma

<u>Psychological</u>

Mental illness (various causes)

Stress

Muscle pain/back pain

Irritable bowel syndrome

Psychosomatic illness (see Mario Martinez)

Negative emotions causing illness

Lack of forgiveness causing problems (e.g. cancer)

Negative programming from society (old people are unhealthy)

Medical cursing/Nocebo

Illness from emotions empathy- taking on for others inadequate emotional boundaries

Illness has some beneficial role for person (e.g. sympathy, control)

<u>Illness is an "illusion"</u>

Belief system. If you believe it, you receive it (e.g. Bruce Lipton Biology of Belief and Cancer).

You make it up by defining it.

<u>Illness as Energy</u>

Release of energies

Assisting in releasing a lot of low vibration energies, e.g. cold or flu.

"Dirty Prana"

Miasms

Chakra problems

Problems with aura

Lacking, or weak, energetic shielding

Need to Earth

Orgone deficiency (Wilhelm Reich)

<u>Illness As Meaning</u>

Every illness is telling you something (e.g. Louis Hay)

It is about personal and spiritual evolution

It means you've drifted off your soul's path

Illness or dis-ease is there to tell us we are out of balance in some area of our lives

Illness as separation from God/source

<u>Intentional Spiritual Harm By Others</u>

Curses

Hexes

Psychic attack

Psychic vampirism

<u>Negative Entities</u>

Demonic possession

Attacked by negative entities

<u>Extraterrestrial causes</u>

Alien (ET) abduction, surgeries/implantations

Shamanic

Soul loss/fragmentation

Power animal loss

Power loss

Planetary influences

Solar flares

Saturn Returns and challenging angles

Harmful Spiritual Growth Practices

Kundalini Syndrome

Conjuring spirits

Other

Healing crisis

Illness as punishment by God

Afterword

"Come out of the circle of time and into the circle of love." ~Rumi

I sincerely hope that you found this book useful and that you were able to use the techniques help improve your life and the life of others. I would love to hear your comments, and constructive criticisms, so please email me at: erichhunterhealing@gmail.com

If you are interested in learning more, please check out my website at www.erichhunter.com

Thank you for reading my book and for circling the square of your life.

Sincerely,

Erich Hunter Ph.D.

About The Author

Dedicated to spiritual and esoteric healing modalities, Erich Hunter Ph.D. has developed a unique synthesis that transforms body, mind, and spirit.

After working for over a decade as a Ph.D. researcher, and award-winning educator in field of the Biological Sciences, he fully awakened to his spiritual path and made a major life transition to follow his calling as a modern day wizard.

Dr. Hunter has studied and practiced many spiritual/energy healing modalities. Eventually, he discovered pendulum healing and found that using the pendulum was a much more effective and fun way for him to carry out his healing work. Over time he has developed his own methods and theoretical foundation for pendulum healing, and now he teaches classes to students from around world about his innovative methods and approach.

He is also the author of "How To Heal With A Pendulum" available as an e-book on Amazon.com.

Bringing the noble spirit of scientific inquiry to his intuitive wizardry, Dr. Hunter merges the best of both worlds with a grounded and compassionate approach. Originally from New York, he now resides with his wife in Ojai, California. He enjoys taking walks in nature, playing with his dog, studying alternative science, and spiritual ceremony.

Circling The Square Of Life Online Class

"Dr. Erich Hunter, with his 'Circling The Square' dowsing techniques is one of the most encouraging, empowering and expandable dowsing courses I've come across to date. And it is offered in such a way that it is valuable for the novice and the experienced dowser alike." --Joyce Decker

Circling the Square of Life: An Online Pendulum Healing Course

Would you like to bring the material in this book to life? Consider taking Dr. Hunter's online course based on this book.

The course includes the following:

- A series of four 1-hour classes (Each topic is pre-recorded video)
- You can e-mail questions to Dr. Hunter
- The class is pre-recorded (so you don't need to attend live)
- Access to the private Facebook Group

A certificate will be awarded upon completion.

For more information visit:

http://www.erichhunter.com/

"This course was beyond all expectations! It's four modules addressed Healing, Abundance and Prosperity, Relationships and Self-Expression. This powerful healing modality was presented in a simple to follow format and empowered us to be better and more effective healers as well as providing

us with the ability to affect and improve different areas of life; personal, communal and world-wide. I am very grateful for Dr. Erich Hunter and for all of his knowledge, wisdom, time and generosity given throughout the course."- Maria Sandoval

"After each lesson, I was able to use the handouts to utilize my pendulum for expanded healing work that I do with Reiki-Acupuncture. The pendulum is such an integrative energetic tool I had not previously included in my healing sessions; however, I get I am learning how valuable this type of healing is....thank you so much. Looking forward to another class!" - Diane Cloud

"I found Erich's style of teaching to be fully engaging & considerate of all, extremely easy, flowing and informative. I have taken many e courses and this is one of the best. I anticipated each week's class with excitement. The course was short yet loaded with extremely helpful knowledge, useful techniques and wisdom Erich offers transformation for a better world that benefits everyone..."under grace and in perfect ways". I highly recommend any teaching or service offered by Erich Hunter. Blessings." --Sharron C.

Printed in Great Britain
by Amazon